WORLD WAR II
as experienced by
a Wehrmacht Heer Soldier

KURT NOACK
Poland, France, Denmark
Yugoslavia, POW

Robert Stephen Spangler
Francis Kurt Spangler

PUBLICATIONS BY DR. ROBERT S. SPANGLER

Texts

Test Manual to Accompany Adolescent Development and the Life Tasks, by Guy Mamaster, MS, Allyn and Bacon, Inc., 1977

(With Dr. Ben F. Eller) Test Manual to Accompany Understanding Adolescence, 3rd Edition by James F. Adams. Boston MS Allyn and Bacon, Inc., 1976

Journal Articles

(With Michael Taylor) "Capital Culpability: Daubert Necessitates Re-Evaluation of Condemned Persons," The Advocate, Vol. 21, Issue 3, May 1999

(With Dr. David A. Sabitino) "Temporal Stability of Gifted Children's Intelligence," Roeper Review, November 1994

(With Dr. Robert G. Shepard) "An Analysis of the Effect of a Vermont Folk Remedy on the Self-Reports of University Students," International Journal of Instructional Media, Vol. 5, No. 5, No. 3, 1977-78, pp 273-275

(With L. Stephen Ward) "Selection or Shaping: A Critical Decision for American Parents," International Journal of Instructional Media, Vol. 5, No. 4, 1977-78, pp 397-401

(With Dr. Robert G. Shepard) "Marijuana: A Phenomenological Synthesis," Mid-South Educational Researcher, November 1976, Vol. 4, No. 3

(With Dr. Norman Hankins) "Comparison of Two Evaluative Procedures on Retention by College Students," Psychological Reports, 1975, pp 36, 613-614

Marijuana Today: Facts for Classroom Teachers and Counselors, A Brief Annotated Bibliography, Johnson City, TN, ETSU Printing Department, August 1975

(With Dr. Charles M. Achilles et al) "Innovations in Higher Education: Approaches to Improved Instruction" (Symposium) Mid-South Educational Researcher, November

1975, Vol. 3, No. 4

(With Dr. Ogden Lindsley, Dr. Henry Pennypacker, et al) <u>The Handbook of Precise Behavior Facts</u>, Kansas City, KS, Precision Media, Inc., June 1971

(With Dr. Donald Avila and Charles Lund) "The Relationship Between Crime and the Criminal's Belief About the Basic Nature of Man," <u>Research Study</u>, pp. 669-69, FL (Florida Division of Corrections), December 1969

PUBLISHED BY DR. R.S. SPANGLER
P.O. Box 340, Horseshoe Beach, Florida 32648

PRINTED IN THE UNITED STATES OF AMERICA

ISBN: 978-1-7364584-0-2 [paperback]

ISBN: 978-1-7364584-1-9 [e-book]

For additional copies, contact Amazon.com.

DEDICATION

Former Oberleutnant Kurt Noack had two requests if the experiences were published: First, his dedication is to the men he served with who were killed, wounded, or missing in action, the 29th Infantry Regiment in Poland, the 323rd Infantry Regiment in France, and the 22nd Infantry in Yugoslavia, and the men of the Verfügungstruppen (Disposition) Unit of the Waffen SS who fought alongside them. They were young elite combat troops trained to fight on the line and nothing else. Secondly, he requested that all of the names, except his, his family, and historical figures, be changed to protect the privacy of the families. We honored both of these requests.

FKS
Vienna, Austria
12 January 2014

CONTENTS

ACKNOWLEDGMENTS

ORIGINAL PHOTO LAYOUT BY CHRISTY SPANGLER
LIBRARY RESEARCH ASSISTANCE BY JASON WILLIAMS
MAP ON PAGE 294 BY CAROL V. SPANGLER
MANUSCRIPT PREPARATION AND FINAL PHOTO LAYOUT
BY THERESA M. SAYLOR
TRANSLATION [ENGLISH/GERMAN] AND EDITOR
THERESA MIDDLETON SAYLOR

SPECIAL THANKS TO DEE DEE PENNINGTON FOR YEARS OF
EXCELLENT PROFESSIONAL ASSISTANCE WITH MY PSYCHOLOGICAL
REPORTS AND THANKS FOR COORDINATION OF THIS EFFORT (RSS)

PREFACE

I arrived in Bremerhaven, Germany, by Troop ship in mid-December, 1964. We were escorted to a troop train and started our journey into the heartland of Germany. The train made many short stops; groups of soldiers got off and were met by a U.S. Army NCO with a clipboard as the train began to move again. As we moved into Germany, I thought about my family heritage and realized that I was probably more German/Irish than any other combination, but I also had French, Spanish, and a small percentage of Native American blood. I looked forward to seeing Germany, France, and Spain since my life was being disrupted by a draft notice in July, 1964, which I ignored and reenlisted. I had been divorced, and that triggered the draft. Seems like my active duty time during the Korean War in the Infantry was a couple of months shy of fulfilling my active duty requirement.

Also, even though I had temporary custody of my two young

children, it only counted if it was permanent custody. My parents agreed to care for my daughter and son while I served again on active duty, this time in the field artillery.

As the train moved ahead, I looked out the window, watching the countryside roll by between small villages and towns. I was shocked to see pristine towns, rebuilt roads and autobahns, and industrious people, older males and women mostly working at their daily tasks. I expected a lot of rubble.

It was only nineteen years since World War II had ended and Germany had been severely damaged. I thought back about four relatives who had fought and served in Europe. My aunt, Eileen B., who was an RN, WAC First Lieutenant, saw more horror than the men on a day by day basis; her husband, my uncle, Bud B., who saw combat as a company grade officer in the infantry; my uncle, Frank A., was a belly gunner on a B17 and completed his required missions over Germany and other targets as the war ended. Then there was my uncle, Webby R., who was in the second or third wave of infantry soldiers who crossed the Remagen Bridge on March 7,

1945. He was seriously wounded when he stepped on an anti-personnel mine eight weeks before the end of World War II.

As a child at my maternal grandparents' house, I used to hide and listen to these combat veterans tell their stories to each other when they thought no one else was listening. That's why, as I looked out of my window on the train, I expected a defeated country with leftover rubble and a sad, depressed group of people, especially since Germany had been divided into East and West. Instead, I was seeing active, smiling, even people waving to us, as the train passed. It was hard to believe how much progress they had made and were still making.

Regardless, I thought that even though we were no longer an Occupation Force, we were still there to protect them from a possible, more likely probable, attack by Soviet Forces through the Fulda Gap, a natural invasion route which had been used by aggressors for over a thousand years.

When I arrived in Frankfurt/Main, I boarded a van which took us to an Army compound in downtown Frankfurt/Main. We all waited until our assigned units came with deuce and a half trucks to pick us up. I enjoyed looking the building over as it was originally a Wehrmacht Heer barracks.

While there, I learned that the building was now under the U.S. Seventh Army. My orders read I was assigned to Battery A, 2nd Battalion, 27th Field Artillery, which was in the Third Armored Division. The operative word in my orders was field. We would spend about one hundred sixty-two days per year in the field, training near the border in the Fulda Region according to the NCOs in Frankfurt/ Main. And they told the truth!

Whenever we returned from the field exercises to Friedberg, Hesse, where our garrison, Ray Barracks, was located, Herr Noack and I worked on the project. He spoke better English than I spoke German, but I understood many more German words than I spoke. If I didn't understand something during our walks, it was explained later to me when we finished our walks and returned to his home. I was restricted to off duty hours, so it was usually dinner, a long walk, and then a drink or two, and return to Ray Barracks. After his daughter, Hannelore Noack, and I were married, I could live off post and we had much more time and my German was improving. We both enjoyed working together; it was cathartic for him and highly informative for me. Our mutual respect grew as we worked together. We completed thirty-five interviews before I rotated back to the United States in late December, 1966.

INTRODUCTION

The story of how former Oberleutnant Kurt Noack's experiences in World War II became published is a short story in its own right. However, we will cut to the chase. The first author conducted thirty-five interviews with Herr Kurt Noack in Friedberg, Hesse, in 1965, 1966, and 1973. The first interview occurred after dinner in Noack's dining room when Herr Noack noticed his wife, Johanna, putting photographs in the trash. He asked what they were about, and she said, "The war." He shrugged and said, "Okay. It's over and young folks aren't interested." The first author interrupted politely and told both Herr and Frau Noack that he cared and he was sure that their grandchildren would also. Herr Noack smiled and asked his wife to remove the photos from the trash and bring over to the dining table. That started the project of annotating the photos, listening to his verbal description of returning to the Army by conscription in 1939, the campaigns he was in, occupation duty in

Denmark, promotion from Hauptfeldwebel to Second Lieutenant and, after completing more legal studies, promotion to Oberleutnant (First Lieutenant), then the final campaign and the end of the war.

The notes, dictations, and photos were stored in a bank safety deposit box in Gainesville, Florida, from May 1967 until September 1972 when they were moved to a bank box in Johnson City, Tennessee, until given to the second author on 29 November 2009 in Alexandria, Virginia. On September 8 and December 12, 2009, both authors and family members, including Herr Noack's daughter, Hannelore Noack Spangler-Freund, materials and tapes were discussed, and it was decided that we should publish her dad's World War II experiences. Valuable comments on Germany civilian living conditions were made by her husband, Karl-Heinz Freund.

The materials were then locked up in the second author's home office in Alexandria, Virginia, as he had become very preoccupied with his career with ATF at their D.C. headquarters, and his wife was equally busy with her career at NTSB in D.C. Herr Noack's daughter and her husband had returned home in Germany.

The first author had retired in 1995 as a Professor of Psychology in the Department of Human Development and Learning at a regional university in Tennessee in order to devote his time to private practice in Cumberland Gap, Tennessee. This allowed appointments for people from three states. He had been in practice as a licensed psychologist since 1982 twenty percent of the time from 1982 until January 1995 and, when he retired from the university in favor of private practice, to one hundred percent of the time.

The materials sat dormant. In September 2011 Herr Karl-Heinz Freund and Frau Hannelore Noack Spangler-Freund returned to the United States for a visit in Pompano Beach, Florida. We all again talked about the materials and rehashed the possibility of a publication. As the second author and his wife, Christy, had moved to South Florida, he had more available time. We talked seriously about starting to put pen to paper.

In September 2012 Herr Fruend and Frau Noack Spangler-Freund visited us again in Pompano Beach, Florida. Eventually after many happy days at the beach and restaurants, the question came:

"How is progress on the book?" We had to report, "No progress," then ordered another beer and bourbon and water. We finally got started reviewing notes, tapes, and photos, starting with Herr Noack's early life and conditions in Germany circa 1935 to 1939.

Well, finally the two authors found themselves in Vienna, Austria, in early January 2014, looking out the hotel window at the Danube. This brought back a lot of memories of former Oberleutnant Noack's experiences during World War II near and on the Sava River (Sau), which flows into the Danube. They sat down over the next few days in Vienna and actually put pen to paper. They hammered out the rough outline and a statement about what Oberleutnant Noack wanted for a dedication and precautions to spare families from an invasion of their privacy. The book was finally in progress.

In September 2019 at the family reunion at Pompano Beach, Florida, minus one, Christy Spangler, widow of Francis Kurt Spangler, second author, turned all materials she located back to the first author. There had been many nighttime phone calls between both authors between January 2014 and March 2019. The first author actually got back to work fleshing out the outline during May 2019 and the book, except for corrections, was completed on April 26, 2020.

2
KURT NOACK'S EARLY LIFE

Kurt Noack was born in Guben, Germany, at the turn of the 20th century. He attended school in Guben and was in the academic track. His grades were above average and he advanced each year without difficulty. From his parents' comments to him, "he had a good future; it was up to him."

Kurt was raised as a Christian by his parents, Gustav and Hanne Noack. He and his little sister, Margarete, were regular churchgoers under the example and supervision of their mother. Later in life his children were baptized as Lutherans, so the assumption is that he too was Lutheran.

Kurt was a high school adolescent when Archduke Franz Ferdinand and his spouse, Sophia, of the Austrian-Hungarian Empire were assassinated in Sarajevo on the 28th of June, 1914. War was declared by the Empire against Serbia. By August, World War I was underway.

Young Kurt sensed the enthusiasm for World War I in his fellow countrymen. He continued his studies and kept up with all the war news. By August 1917 he appeared fully grown and full of boyhood dreams of being a soldier for his Fatherland. To the silent dismay of his mother but after talking to her father, Herr Mileus Juelich, with her husband out of town, she signed a paper stating that he had turned seventeen in August 1917 and that his birth certificate was to follow when his father returned home. Kurt enlisted at the end of August 1917 into the Reichswehr Heer.

By the time Herr Noack returned home, it was too late. Kurt was a soldier. His birth certificate never followed, nor was it requested.

Kurt Noack began to become a Heer Private (Grenadier/Schutze). After graduation he went straight to his unit at the front in Belgium. He remained in Belgium, taking part in multiple engagements, until the war ended.

Within a few weeks he was allowed to return home in Guben.

After all the treaties were implemented, he finally received an Honorable Discharge and returned to his academic studies. His objective test scores opened the door to the police academy in Sondershausen/Thuerngen. After a series of on and off jobs, he entered and graduated from the police academy in 1924.

Before going to the police academy, like thousands of other German patriots who served in World War I, Herr Noack took his birth certificate and school records to a government office and had his date of birth corrected, stating, "must have been a typo in 1917." The clerk smiled and nodded in the affirmative. He served as a police officer during the Weimar Republic until 1933. This is when the Third Reich began.

Being so far east, Guben is very close to Poland. Herr Kurt Noack had opined that he had not noticed much change for several years except that there was improved hope for economic stability and a better life. One prevalent rumor did worry citizens and open-minded police officers. It was the story being told in private that, if you were caught behaving in an inappropriate manner, "the Gestapo would come and get you."

After serving under the Third Reich for three years as a police officer following his nine years with the Weimar Republic, he was told by his supervisor that there would be no promotion slots for him for several years. Having been married in early 1934, he thought long and hard but decided to resign from the police department in 1936 and study law for a year while working a government job in administration in Calau. This made it possible to prepare for a good future while supporting his wife and young son, Hans-Jürgen. At the end of the year the Noacks moved to Cottbus. With law school transcripts and twelve years of police experience being considered, he was promoted to a Town Magistrate for traffic offenses and other minor disputes. He worked long hours diligently in 1937, 1938, and through July of 1939. He was beginning to relax as he was beginning his middle age years; he felt sure that he and his family had a secure future. However, as many Ausländers say, "he had another think coming."

At the end of July, 1939, Herr Noack was sent to

Frankfurt/Oder to handle official business for the government.

He arrived home on Saturday in time for supper. After talking with his wife, Johanna, and after playing with his young son, Hans-Jürgen, they retired. Sunday morning Johanna gave the mail that had accumulated while he was in Frankfurt/Oder. He sorted through the pile, placing unimportant mail to the side; his wife could deal with it. He read the business mail and other mail he considered important. He then spent the day resting and interacting with Johanna and Hans-Jürgen. After supper he looked at office matters and his agenda for the week. He made a decision to shift non-urgent cases from Monday to Tuesday and telephoned his clerk.

On Monday, 31 July 1939, Herr Noack went to his office and had his staff finish notifying individuals of the new dates and times for their hearings. The two urgent cases would be heard that afternoon. Like others, he enjoyed the walk home for lunch, planning to review the two afternoon cases while having his lunch.

FAMILY PHOTOS

Kurt Noack, age 4, with family in Guben

Wedding photo: Kurt and Johanna Nufek, Thuringen, Germany

Weimar police officers gassing up on way to meeting with Hungarian police

At Border, 1930; Noack and fellow officers

Arriving at conference

After police conference

3

UPROOTED: BACK TO BERLIN

Monday morning looked like a nice summer day. He smelled coffee and the breakfast Johanna was preparing. He also heard Hans-Jürgen trying to get another brötchen with butter and strawberry jam. He had a pleasant breakfast and said goodbye to Hans-Jürgen and his wife. He promised he would pick up some produce she had listed on his way home for lunch. Herr Noack then set out for work at his usual brisk pace.

On arriving at his government office, he checked with his chief clerk that he had instructed the night before to reschedule the non-urgent cases for Tuesday. His clerk told him it was all handled with no problem.

After writing explanations of why the first three non-urgent cases were not heard, he spent the rest of the morning doing busy work and started looking at the two afternoon cases. He left the office a little early for lunch so he could stop at the produce market about two blocks away. He selected vegetables, paid, and headed home at a slower pace, stopping to buy a newspaper and greet friends that he passed on the sidewalk.

When he arrived home, his wife had put Hans-Jürgen in bed for a nap so it would be quiet for lunch. He handed her the produce and took the newspaper into the dining room and sat down. After a drink of water, he went into the kitchen and washed his hands and then reseated himself in the dining room. His wife had placed his hot tea and onion soup with cold cuts, cheese, and bread on the table. While he was finishing his meal, Johanna brought in a small piece of hot apple strudel and refilled his teacup.

Looking tense, Joanna asked, "Did you read the letter from the S.D. (the State Secret Police staffed by the political S.S. and the Gestapo) I gave you Sunday?"

After wiping his mouth with the cloth napkin, he responded, "Yes, I did."

She inquired, "What are you doing about it?" He told his highly concerned wife, who was tearing up, "It's a mistake. I'm almost forty years old and I'm a combat veteran from World War I. I have all my military papers, including my discharge. Also, after leaving the police department, I let myself get out of shape. I don't think they want me. Why do you seem so concerned over an obvious mistake?"

Now tearful, Johanna sat down at the dining table and stated, "While you were at your office this morning , two S.S. officers stopped by and said they would return after lunch and that you would be going with them to Berlin today; either to the Wehrmacht Heer or to prison, it was your choice." Weeping, she said that she had packed his bag as instructed by the two S.S. officers and "they are waiting outside."

Kurt smirked and replied, "Let them in. I'll talk to them. Surely it's a mistake. After all, I'm a traffic Magistrate in this town. Don't worry so much."

Johanna showed the S.D. representatives in and seated them

in the dining room. She brought in coffee and left, closing the door.

The S.S. officers sipped their coffee and politely listened to Herr Magistrate Noack explain his position. When he finished, the Senior Officer said, "We commend you for your current service and your service in World War I; however, the Reich is recalling and conscripting men under age thirty-five, and all abled-bodied men ages thirty-five to fifty-two, regardless of current positions or past service, especially if they have police experience or law school, and you have both. You are needed in countries we may occupy and need to be retrained briefly to be ready to serve. With your education, police experience, and family status, you will be paid as a Master/Sergeant (Stabsfeldwebel) during training. You have thirty minutes to call your office and explain you will be relieved by a much older Magistrate by Berlin. Say goodbye to your family and meet us at the staff car." They politely left.

The self-assured Magistrate Kurt Noack appeared shaken to his soul but had a stiff upper lip and assurances for his wife and child. He promised to bring Hans-Jürgen a nice toy from Berlin shortly. Johanna did her best to appear happy, but little Hans-Jürgen knew something was not right. They waved goodbye as he was driven away to Berlin.

Former Magistrate Noack looked back through the rear window and did his best to smile and wave at his family. As they drove toward Berlin, it finally sank in on him. He was no longer a respected Traffic Magistrate but a middle-aged Master/Sergeant entering retraining at the Berlin Training and Retraining Center.

When he reported in at the center, the two S.S. Officers received a signature for him from the officer on duty and left. He was given bedding, basic uniform items, and boots and was told there would be a brief welcome formation at 2200 hours in the gym.

He was then taken to his assigned room which he would share with another recalled middle-aged man who had arrived the day before. His roommate was very helpful, and by formation they both fell in appropriately dressed.

4

RETRAINING: FROM REICHSWEHR HEER

TO WEHRMACHT HEER

Master/Sergeant Noack soon found that most of the other middle-aged recalled former soldiers were in disbelief like he was, but within a few days they fell into the routine of P.T., classes, and drills. Wearing the new uniform, they were learning to care for and use the new model weapons that were a big improvement on the weapons in World War I. The Table of Organization and Equipment (T, O & E) of World War II was very different and required much study as was the Chain of Command. They trained and studied, and Master/Sergeant Noack excelled. The most boring tasks was learning all the forms required to be completed at the different levels of command, Company, Battalion, Brigades, Divisions, Armies, Corps, OKH, and OKW. The most enjoyable activity was firearm training; learning to use and become skilled with each new weapon.

Due to their age and past experience and comments from their retraining officers, most retrainees knew they would be serving at some level in administration. However, they understood, like all soldiers in all armies, that their basic duty was as an infantryman. If their unit was in a bind, they would be needed in the trenches or needed to replace a fallen leader if they were next in line by rank. It was understood.

Young trainees at Berlin Training Center. A few hours off at the center; no passes yet. A few days from graduation; becoming a Wehrmacht Heer soldier August 1939.

Middle-aged Kurt Noack congratulated by Berlin Training Officer after his graduation; rank of Stahsfeldwebel (Master/Sergeant). He received his orders to the 29th Infantry Regiment in late August 1939, promoted again when he arrived at the 29th Infantry Headquarters.

He was assigned to the 6th Company 2nd Battalion of the 29th Infantry Regiment. On the 31st of August, he was promoted to Sgt/Major (Hauptfeldwebel). They moved out toward Poland on September 1, 1939, in response to a Polish attack on a German radio station and in newspapers at the end of August. This was being reported on German radio stations and newspapers.

The 29th Infantry Regiment boarded a troop train from Guben to Schneidmusehle; detrained and started marching east to Gurdziady on September 1, 1939. This is when their first battle against the Polish army occurred.

A few days from graduation, become a Wehrmacht Heer soldier, August 1939

5

MOVING INTO POLAND

Unknown to Sgt/Major (Hauptfeldwebel) Noack and all Wehrmacht Heer Units moving toward Poland on 1st of September, 1939, the attack by Poland on Germany on the 30th of August had been a fake attack orchestrated by the S.D. in Berlin. Most did not learn this until years later.

Since the 29th Infantry Regiment was assigned to the Kaserne in Guben, which is very close to the Polish border as established in 1918, the 29th Infantry Regiment was among the first units to see combat in Poland. Hauptfeldwebel (Sgt/Major) Noack recalled, "We didn't see any dead German soldiers until we reached Konitz. The men in the 6th Company, 2nd Battalion, 29th Infantry Regiment were brought into this stark reality after having seen a young Panzer Commander who was half out of his Panzer, dead and burning with his Panzer. The sight and smell of burning flesh was a first for the young soldiers. They now had their baptism." He added, "From the border to Konitz we had suffered many minor wounds and injuries, but this was the first death of one of us, and the fact it was an officer really drove in the realization of our mortality."

From Konitz he reported, "We moved east and then south for two days, encountering sporadic attacks and picking up Polish soldiers surrendering en route. They gave up all weapons but were allowed to keep their other gear. Moving in the direction of Warsaw with POWs in tow, we were occasionally attacked, especially when near rural towns and particularly when halted to give our troops and POWs a brief rest. Old men, men, boys, and women would scream at us as we took our breaks; this was ignored and sometimes the POWs would shout warnings to them. Unfortunately, on more than one occasion as we moved closer to Warsaw, the emotionally disturbed and outraged civilians would run at us with pitchforks, axes, butcher knives, and clubs. The POWs would shout, but they were so enraged they kept coming. Our young troops had standing orders to shout one warning shot to drop their weapon; if they kept coming with their weapon, they could fire. Some young soldiers obeyed, but some faced with their own possible death just fired when they saw them coming at them. The ones that had non-life-threatening wounds were treated by one of our team of medics and a POW medic, then left behind as we moved out." Those with serious wounds were left for civilian evacuation to local doctors.

"On our march toward Warsaw we saw the bombed out small airfields and no Polish Air Force in the skies. Also, the Polish Army resistance was diminishing rapidly as we picked up more and more surrendering Polish soldiers."

In late September, prior to reaching Warsaw, the 29th Infantry Regiment was ordered to stop and turn over all POWs to a detail en route to us. Then we were to stand in place until further orders, staying alert, and to defend our position, no retreat.

Poland's surrender was accepted on the 27th day of September, 1939, but the Warsaw Garrison managed to fight to the 28th day of September, showing gallantry defending their country.

The 29th Infantry Regiment was ordered to move back to

their Kaserne in Guben, Germany, on the 27th day of September and were en route home when the Polish Garrison fell in Warsaw.

The Soviets moved in and claimed about half of Poland, firing very few shots and suffering very few casualties. The Wehrmacht Heer, Waffen SS, and Luftwaffe had about 10,500 killed and another thirty-six thousand wounded as well as three thousand missing. Polish losses were much worse, but the Soviet's losses were less than one hundred, and they were allowed to occupy the Eastern half of Poland.

On a micro-level, Hauptfeldwebel Noack had reported that the 2nd Battalion of the 29th Infantry Regiment lost twelve killed in action, one hundred were wounded, and none were missing. Noack's assessment of the Polish Campaign was: "Poland did not have a modern Army. No shortage of brave men, but horse cavalry cannot face Panzers. It was crazy. Their government should have negotiated for peace the day we entered Poland." Of course, at that time, he and other Germans did not know that Germany had not been invaded by Poland in late August 1939. It had been a faked attack planned and executed by the SD on a German radio station.

6

RETURN WEST AND THE LONG WAIT

On the route back to Germany, the 29th Infantry Regiment stopped at Radom in East Central Poland for supplies and replacements that had been en route before the surrender, and then the pleasure of transit back to their Kaserne in Guben, Germany.

This was a great gift for Sgt/Major Kurt Noack as his family was in Cottbus, less than an hour away by motorcycle from the Kaserne in Guben. With his rank and diligent work habits he could fit in a quick trip home when his work was completed a few times per month.

After all were accounted for and the normal Heer routines were reestablished, the wounded were sent home to recuperate. Even though his 2nd Battalion had one of the lowest casualty rates, he found their morale low. This bothered him, but he knew the answer: keep them too busy to think about the recent past experience. Noack wore out his company clerks making and changing the weekly training schedules that were consistent with the weekly Battalion schedule, but added extra time tearing down and reassembling their weapons and extra time for P.T. and the firing range. He also added an evening session to familiarize them with Allied Infantry weapons and recognition of enemy armor and aircraft. Morale improved and his Company Commander was pleased.

About twice per month he was allowed a pass to go home for twenty-four hours using a Battalion motorcycle. He knew the worst was yet to come and did his best to have the troops in the 6th Company, 2nd Battalion physically fit and ahead of other troops on the rifle range. Their excellent familiarity with enemy weapons in case some day they needed to pick them up and defend themselves and Kameraden with allied weapons helped to improve morale. He thought to himself, "Age sure as hell has physical disadvantages, but it has given you experience that can save your life and the lives of men depending on you."

He remained in his position with the 29th Infantry Regiment until the early spring of 1940 while also enjoying his time on a few weekends per month with his wife, Johanna, and growing son, Hans-Jürgen.

Zugfuehrer Noack, center, with a superior officer
(right front) in Black Forest on the way to Rhine and
 France, May 1940

Officers and men of 323rd Infantry Regiment the
afternoon before their crossing the Rhine into France,
15 May 1940, early morning

7

INVASION OF FRANCE: DEJA VU

In the Spring of 1940 he was transferred to the Second Company, First Battalion, the 323rd Infantry Regiment and promoted to the rank of Zugfuehrer. This is not a regular rank but is above the highest NCO rank although below the rank of Second Lieutenant (Leutnant). However, the duties were the same as a Second Lieutenant, platoon leader, and only reports to the Company Commander as do other Junior officers. Zugfuehrer Noack was made the Commander of three groups, platoon size. He and his men were sent to Magdeburg for training for several weeks and then returned to the 323rd Infantry Regiment Kaserne.

The 323rd Infantry Regiment was fine tuning its units during the first ten days of May, 1940, for a return to combat. Zugfuehrer Noack worked night and day to get his three groups or detachment ready. Some had seen brief combat, but many were virgins. Now, as an officer, he was not going to lighten up on supervision.

On the 12th day of May, 1940, the 323rd Infantry Regiment boarded a troop train to Freudenstadt, then a forced march at night to the French border. They stayed camouflaged in the woods during the day (good training for later). By the 15th day of May they crossed the Rhine River into the Alsace region of France. As many Germans lived in Alsace, France and Germany had fought for it before, it was still considered German by many residents and German citizens.

Early on the morning of 15 May 1940 in the poorest lighted area near Freiburg they put their rubber rafts and small boats into the Rhine and crossed into France. Some small German artillery units stayed on the German side of the Rhine providing smoke cover. France and England had declared war against them in 1939 in support of Poland so entry into France was not unexpected by French troops. The French Partisans were also ready.

The 323rd Infantry crossed into Alsace and began their march into the Alsace region with minor opposition at first, then increasing resistance from a French withdrawal action, and sporadic partisan gunfire. They were retreating faster than we were advancing. We had to fight their rear guard and partisans to catch up to their main body.

As Zugfuehrer Noack passed a small church, he thought, "this is at least the third time German soldiers have passed this way trying to get our citizens and territory back; how many of us will be wounded or killed this time?" He took a snapshot of the church and said a silent prayer for his troops and himself. He had no time to get a camera before Poland but made sure he had several this time with plenty of film in his detachment's supplies.

The 323rd Infantry Regiment moved slowly into France and up a mountain near Kayserberg with the French troops and partisans falling back as fast as they could. We had sporadic engagement with their troops with some in red pants, making easy targets in the terrain as well as with partisan snipers who was not very good at camouflage.

About ten days of this type of action moving toward the

adjoining region known as Lorraine (Alsace/Lorraine), the 323rd was halted in place and officers and Senior NCOs were ordered to come to the rear for a meeting. Zugfuehrer Noack made sure his men knew to have double well-armed perimeter guards over their area at all times and to rotate breaks with new guards every hour and then joined the others with his senior detachment NCO.

When they all returned to the front lines, the officers and NCOs discovered that two squads in another battalion had failed to have adequate perimeter guards, having only two. The rest of the two squads had stacked their rifles near the shore of a tributary, stripped off their uniforms, and went swimming. These soldiers were between seventeen to twenty years of age. French partisans had cut the throats of the two guards and shot and killed all in the water and on shore.

After all their IDs were documented, they were buried together in a mass grave. The Chaplain said the usual prayers at graveside and some Germans who lived in the closest town which was under Heer control were kind enough to bring flowers. Only one Wehrmach Heer helmet was left to mark the mass grave. A few of the male German civilians promised to stay in touch if they found out which partisan group killed the solders. It was a sad night.

Noack thought to himself as he prepared to sleep that night with adequate guards, "Those kids still thought it was all a game and they called time out. War doesn't work that way."

In less than six weeks the French surrendered. Later they signed the surrender in the same town that Germany had surrendered in 1918; Compiegne, on 22 September 1940.

As of the French surrender, Belgium surrendered, and Holland had already surrendered. Denmark had given up on the day the German troops stepped foot into Denmark to avoid needless deaths and injuries. With British support, Norway fought on for about two months but surrendered on 10 June 1940.

This was heady stuff for the young officers and NCOs, but the older officers and NCOs who had been defeated in 1918 thought it wise to just take one day at a time and stress preparedness.

The 323rd Infantry Regiment along with other units were

ordered to stand in place until further orders to transition into occupation duty were issued. After Zugfuehrer Noack and his detachment were assigned quarters, they received new orders which would require them to arrange movement of supplies from Germany to Colmar, France. Colmar is in Alsace and is a beautiful town. On the Rhine, it was perfect for a supply depot and transportation hub.

Noack and his detachment wasted no time setting up routes from Germany into France and to all future sites that would need supplies on a precise timetable. Noack and his men were ordered to stay on running the Colmar Supply Center and Transportation System.

The rest of the 323rd Infantry Regiment was ordered to Saarbruchen on foot. This took a while. After reaching this destination, they had orders waiting in mid-July to board a troop train to the outskirts of Berlin. In their honor they were to get rested and cleaned up and then march into Berlin with citizens cheering them on 19 July 1940. After this, they would march into Spandau which at that time was a large military training center. Later it became the prison that housed famous former Senior officers convicted by the Allied Court at Nuremberg.

Prior to Noack and his men rejoining the 323rd Infantry in late August, 1940, they were inspected at the supply center by Reichschancellor Adolph Hitler personally. They passed inspection!

323rd Infantry Squad sets up in Alsace

323rd Infantry, May 1940, on a one hour break after moving 30 km in Alsace

323rd Infantry Soldiers escorting French POWs to drop off point

Setting up a crew served weapon in France

323rd Infantry and POWs in France taking a brief break

With an adequate perimeter guard, Officers enjoyed a break in Alsace. France having surrendered, the partisans were now the resistance.

Church in Alsace that made Zugfuehrer Noack think about past wars in Alsace

MEMORIAL TO NAIVETE

A mass grave in Alsace for two squads of teenaged Wehrmacht soldiers. Failing to post an alert twelve armed perimeter guards as trained, while NCOs and officers were all called back to temporary headquarters, these adolescents only had two perimeter guards with rifles. Twenty adolescents stacked their rifles, stripped off their uniforms, and went swimming in an Alsace stream. French partisans that they had been warned about killed the two guards first and then shot the other eighteen. A sad Zugfuehrer even years later, said, "They just didn't understand that this was war, not a game."

8

COMMAND MARCH INTO BERLIN AND SPANDAU

As the 323rd Infantry Regiment marched into Berlin, the cheering crowds were well orchestrated by those in charge, but it really wasn't necessary as the area citizens were very pleased and proud of their soldiers. Alsace had been a bitter pill since 1918 among Germans and this was their time to celebrate. News inside Germany was tightly controlled. All print news and radio had to be approved or shut down, and only information that had been tightly screened and shaped to not conflict with government plans was allowed. However, the average citizen was content, enjoying full employment, adequate income, good healthcare, and autobahns that were second to none. Herr Porsche had complied with Reich

Chancellor Hitler's order to produce a car all families could afford. Five years after the Third Reich began, the first Volkswagens started rolling off the production line in 1938. To the mind-set of the great majority of citizens, it was as Voltaire had said in a satire, "It was the best of all possible worlds," albeit for a while.

Not unlike the Roman Emperor Nero of the Julio-Claudian Dynasty who easily controlled Roman citizens with "bread and circuses," Adolph Hitler knew what kept his citizens under strict control but happy, content, and productive.

After leaving Spandau on July 20, 1940, the 323rd Infantry Regiment was stationed at a training center in Döbertiz. Noack and his men joined them in August.

323rd Infantry staff car in Berlin after their march in Berlin parade and into Spandau, July 19, 1940.

Members of the 323rd Infantry squad waiting to be called to attention in Döbertiz area. They were there for replacements, re-supply and new orders.

When the men of the 323rd Infantry received their orders, Zugfuehrer Noack was surprised to be transferred to Denmark with his detachment for occupation duty.

Zugfruehrer Noack and some of his men in route to Denmark for occupation duty; Winter 1941.

After arriving by ship in Denmark, they moved through several towns until April, 1941, then went to Jute until July, 1941 and then he went on to Tonder. Finally, being settled in, everything changed! "Operation Barbarossa" had started on June 22, 1941.

All younger officers, NCOs, and soldiers were to be transferred to the Eastern front while all older officers, NCOs. and soldiers were to be transferred to Denmark and other occupied countries. Middle-aged Zugfuehrer Noack alone was transferred to the Kammandantur in Kolding, Denmark. He bid farewell to his

men and left for Kolding.

Noack with officers and German civilians who lived in Denmark in 1942

Noack's staff at Kammandantur in Kolding, Denmark. Photos sent to him after his transfer with warm personal note from his men. Note that they all are unarmed in front of their office building.

9

ORDERED TO DENMARK FOR OCCUPATION DUTY

From August 1940 through January 1941, Zugfuehrer Noack and his detachment were in training for the fine details of working with and supervising a civilian government and what documented information must be classified and forwarded to Berlin. During February, the 323rd Infantry had Kaserne duty while short leaves home were rotated among the enlisted men, the NCOs, and officers.

During March 1941, the 323rd Infantry Regiment was transported to Warnemunda in Rostock, Germany, on the Baltic Sea along with the 218th Infantry Regiment by train and then by ship to the small port town of Gedser, Denmark. Here the 323rd Infantry Regiment and the 218th Infantry Regiment split up. The 323rd went to Korsor just below Halsskov, Denmark. Troops slept in schools and at a hotel. In late April, the 323rd Infantry Regiment went to Jutland, rested, and then on to Tonder, Denmark, in July.

While the 323rd Infantry was integrating into the occupation duties required in Tonder, "Operation Barbarossa" had started with the invasion of Russia. The Wehrmacht Heer and Waffen SS needed all younger soldiers, NCOs, and officers on the Russian front. Older soldiers, NCOs, and officers were transferred to occupation duty in the various countries being occupied at that time, and the younger men were on their way to German units needing replacements. At the end of July, 1941, Zugfuehrer Noack had his Senior NCO gather his detachment for an informal party to say goodbye as he had orders transferring him alone to the Kammandantur in Kolding. The party was a nice, although bittersweet, farewell to all who had shared so much together. The old solider who had taught them so much was going to Kolding, and most of his men would probably be replacements headed back into deadly combat. They promised to stay in touch, and he and his men said, "Auf Weidersehen."

After reporting for duty in Kolding, he was briefed on his duties and met his new staff. After a week or so, he was familiar with all of his duties and, as usual, studied all the relevant regulations that controlled his duties and personal behavior. Within two weeks he and his small staff were working well and he was now calling the shots. His duties included billeting incoming troops and being one of the liaison officers meeting with civilian Danish officials. He was also responsible for all classified materials of Wehrmacht Heer matters from August 1941 through August 1943.

"Operation Barbarossa" had faced the Wehrmacht with heavy losses in snow and ice not unlike Napoleon in a prior century. They had started too late due to political considerations in Berlin. The operation ceased.

This meant that the occupation sites were getting some younger troops with clerical skills or specialty skills again. His staff was well trained and running smoothly, as were his relationships with Danish civilian officials. When asked about Jewish residents in Denmark in 1966, during one of the interviews, he stated, "To the best of my knowledge there were between seven and eight thousand Jewish citizens in Denmark during my two years there. I do not recall any incidents involving them during my time there. Had there been any movement of any group of Danish citizens from Denmark, I would have seen the required paperwork and classified it. None crossed my desk."

As with all armies and probably across history, when things are going smoothly, watch out! It was time to transfer again!

Zugfuehrer Noack had remarked many times that his time in Denmark (1941-1943) was safe and pleasant duty. He stated that his relationships and official business with Danish businessmen and political officials were mutually respectful. He found these individuals to be good natured and cooperative. He enjoyed working with them in order to carry out his duties.

Fall 1941 Kolding Headquarters. From left, 1st seated, Zugfuehrer Noack

Commander's dinner, Fall 1941 Kolding Denmark; Noack 2nd back from center

Same dinner, Fall 1942, 1st far left is Zugfuehrer Noack

Staff party, Kolding; Seated far right is Zugfuehrer Noack

Drinks with the Commander, Kolding, Winter 1941. First seated on right
Zugfuehrer Noack

Officer and NCO dinner, fall 1942. Noack said, "Always last to leave the party." Noack seated on right.

Barracks party, enlisted, NCOs, and Zugfuehrer Noack (seated at head of table), Denmark, Kolding, 1942

Party for Officer in white jacket, 20 September 1942, Kolding Denmark

Commander dinner in Kolding, Denmark, 26 August 1941

Soldiers of the 323rd infantry regiment arrive in Tonder, Denmark, June 1941

10

BACK TO SCHOOL

In August, 1943, Zugfuehrer Kurt Noack was commissioned as a Second Lieutenant. He was transferred to school in Frankfurt on the Oder for more legal training in military law. With his past law school and traffic magistrate experience, it was a welcome return to the law, and it gave him time to forget about his close call during the train trip en route to Hamburg and Frankfurt/Oder. The train had become a target of opportunity for the U.S. Army Air Corps' B17s. Their bombs jarred the train and shrapnel caused some minor injuries, but the train made it to its destination.

After graduation, Noack was promoted to First Lieutenant (Oberleutnant) and allowed a brief leave to visit his family in Cottbus, which had now grown with the birth of his daughter,

Hannelore Heidi Brigitte, on 4 May 1941.

After a great, albeit short, homecoming, Oberleutnant Noack left en route to the 451st Replacement Company in Germany to do legal work for troops that were en route to the fronts. Again, this meant that he would be able to have his family visit during off duty hours but rarely would he be able to get home for twenty-four hours.

11

TRANSFER TO ATHENS AND CRETE

Oberleutnant Noack was finally assigned to the 22nd Infantry Division as a legal officer. In June, 1944, shortly after D-Day, he was transferred with the 22nd Infantry Division to Crete but was allowed a stop in Athens for ten days to obtain new officer uniforms and materials that he would need for his legal work. He noted the highest security he had seen so far during World War II. He also noted low morale among the troops who were highly restricted.

In July, 1944, he was sent on temporary duty to Frankfurt/Main to represent seventeen enlisted Wehrmacht Heer soldiers who had been convicted of being AWOL during the sentencing phase of their trial. Prosecution was demanding the death penalty. He could not visit his family as he had too much work to do in order to give the AWOL soldiers a fighting chance to escape the death penalty. However, over one weekend, his wife, Johanna, was able to arrive by train for a one day visit, bringing photos of Hannelore and Hans-Jürgen. This break was just what he needed to escape the stress of military life and his responsibility to the seventeen convicted soldiers pending sentence.

He returned to his interviews of each man and study of their combat history and commendations. Oberleutnant Noack made an impassioned plea for mercy for these men who had served with gallantry during combat and were disturbed emotionally by the death and destruction they had witnessed. All seventeen were spared from the death sentence although they did get stiff sentences in a military prison. Noack had done his job well. He packed up his legal papers and luggage and returned to Crete by military air transport.

12

DUTY ON CRETE

When Noack arrived back at the 22nd Infantry Division, he found that his clerks had a solid list of scheduled appointments for him with troops who needed Wills and also other legal matters that needed to be completed. He kept busy trying to get the young troops' legal needs in good shape. He remained very busy into the fall, September, 1944.

13

INTO YUGOSLAVIA: IN HARMS' WAY

All officers were called to the division headquarters for a briefing by the Division Commander according to Noack's memory. He gave the overview, telling them that all heavy weapons and most supplies would be left on Crete. They were allowed one small bag for personal items and uniforms with sidearms. Troops would be limited to the specified uniforms and light weapons assigned to them or their squads. Troops, NCOs, and Company grade officers would be flying out on Junker transports that afternoon. The whole division would arrive at a military airfield in Athens by that evening. Supplies and ammo would be issued later in Thessaloniki, Greece. Troops would be fed at the airfield and billeted for a short time before they boarded a troop train for an overnight trip to Thessaloniki later that month. After getting ammo for all light weapons and other supplies, they would march north and encamp in an isolated area prior to beginning their mission. This would be a fast moving entry into Yugoslavia just to the west and north of Kilkis.

The Division Commander stated, "Our object is not territory but finding pockets of Wehrmacht soldiers near Skopje, Prishtina, and below Kragujevac that are trapped. We will move to the east side of the Vardar River and move in accordance with information from our Recon NCOs. We will assess the size of enemy troops surrounding our soldiers and attack with more than adequate force to open up a pathway for our men while the rest of the Division continues to move on toward the next objective. We will be fighting Communist partisans, Tito's troops, and the possibility of Soviet advisors, maybe other troops as it is reported by OKH that Soviets are moving through Bulgaria and Romania. After we reach and free our last group, we will move as fast as possible away from their troops toward Visegrád. It is safe, and then to Sarajevo for hospitalization of the wounded, supplies, and new orders from our Corps Commander."

The Commander went on, from Noack's recollection, "All officers with non-combat positions are now being reassigned according to their ranks to Company or Battalion positions. Your orders will be delivered in Athens at the airstrip. When you get your new assignments, immediately report to your new Commander for instructions and billeting." The Division Commander wished them well and said, "See you in Athens."

After being dismissed, Oberleutnant Noack took his one small suitcase to Division Headquarters for transport with them to the large Junker tri-engine transport. He realized as he boarded the Junker transport that he had forgotten his camera and film. He was angry at himself for about a minute. He wondered what his orders would be. Regardless of what your specialty is, all soldiers know that in combat they are basic infantry soldiers first; their specialty is first when not in combat. Naturally an officer has to be ready to assume command if his Commander is killed or unable to function and he is the highest ranking officer. Noack received his orders at the airstrip in Athens and reported to the Battalion and Company he was assigned as second in command. His new commanding officer was a young Captain (Hauptmann) with minimal combat experience but cordial and in private said he was happy to have a seasoned combat veteran with him.

At the end of September, 1944, they boarded the train. The overnight train ride was non-eventful. They detrained and saw food waiting for them. After eating, they had an hour to relax before moving out on their march to the isolated camouflaged encampment northwest toward the border. Their Battalion had been in the middle of all of the units in the Division marching toward their camp. Here they would issue ammo to individuals and squads with crew-served weapons like mortars and three man machine gun (MG42) squads. On arrival they were assigned pre-erected tents with sleeping bags. The tents would be left behind and removed by a detail from Athens, who would make sure the area was returned to pristine condition so no one could tell a division had been encamped there.

Noack took charge of the company while the Commander attended multiple meetings over the next three or four days with the

Battalion officers. He met with Company NCOs and ordered them to have all weapons recleaned and inspected by them. He told them to pay close attention to the machine guns and mortars and to make damn sure the men carrying the limited supply of Panzerfausts knew how to handle and fire them if they encounter enemy armor or fortified positions. The NCOs knew without asking that he was a combat veteran and this eased their concerns. He also went through the area giving the troops pointers on keeping their weapons in top operating condition at all times.

The Division started moving toward Yugoslavia on Sunday, 8 October 1944. It was a clear day with temperatures in the mid-fifties. Scouts from the First Brigade called back Recon info to the 22nd Infantry Division Operations Officer. He relayed the info to all Brigades, who passed it down to Battalions and Companies. We were on the Prod by 0700 moving as ordered, locked and loaded.

Thanks to the great work by the Recon advance men, which was rotated between the Brigades every two or three days, this ensured alertness. We avoided needless enemy contact by holding up or doing wide serpentine movements. Many unnecessary small engagements were avoided. After word spread that we were in their domain, the Partisans, Tito's troops, and turncoat Bulgarian soldiers were on the Prod for us. From this time on we were engaging small platoon to company sized attacks and repelling them. By the time their reinforcements arrived, we were gone. Their dead and wounded waited on them and would tie them up for at least a few hours, enabling us to increase our distance from them.

After pushing the enemy back, our first big engagement at Dojoransko near a lake, we sped up on our movement toward Skopje with the Vardar on our west side. Our plan for all three target areas for rescuing pockets of our men or any other pockets of men we found were the same: hit the enemy with a larger force, then move toward the next pocket of troops and then to our line of safety, the Drina River. We would move into the entrapped men with the number of Companies or Battalions needed on the left and right to overwhelm the enemy soldiers.

There was another group of Partisans, the Royal supporters

who had been allied with us, but as they understood that their future was Tito, not Royalty, they were no longer trustworthy. They had helped the Allies recently but there was no way to know how they were going to act on a given day, so if we ran into them, we were cautioned to avoid contact if possible but be prepared to fight.

While moving in to the entrapped soldiers, two groups would push back the enemy, making a corridor to our Division, which was continuing to move slowly north. The last Brigade would have Battalions guarding the rear from the east and south after all soldiers with supplies that we could carry, and other supplies would be blown up and burned. The rescued soldiers would be assisted to integrate into our formation with assistance from Medics and our soldiers. The last Brigade would fight a withdrawing action as we moved out toward our next specified town or city area.

After Dojoransko we fought our way to Skopje in day to day skirmishes until we finally reached Skopje in early November, 1944. Our plan of action worked with heavy fighting for four days until the corridor was wide enough and safe with the exception of the retreating sniper fire. By the fifth day the 22nd Division was on the way toward Prishtina with Division Headquarters having moved up to join in between the last two brigades. Naturally the last brigade was in a defensive posture protecting the rear from attack. On the way to Prishtina we saw discarded trash from their main forces. They seemed to split into two main bodies, one going toward Belgrade and one toward Albania. We didn't know what they were doing, but it was a good sign as we headed to our next objective.

By the time we got to Prishtina, with occasional skirmishes en route, it was late November with colder temperatures becoming a factor, but we used the same tactics as planned. Practice makes perfect, and we were able to rescue our men, along with supplies, faster. We were back en route to our last area below Belgrade behind one of the enemy's large forces for what turned into very heavy combat as we found our last pocket of Wehrmacht soldiers near Kragujevac. Our men were surrounded by well-trained Yugoslavian troops that had fought alongside the Soviets (Russians) as well as large groups of Communist partisans filling in the weakest areas in their lines. We moved through dense forest areas into the outskirts of the small city and fought it out with the largest force we had encountered. With all brigades engaged in the same type of operation to free our men, we were finally successful, but both sides had significant casualties. After getting all identifications of our dead, we moved westward, fighting a withdrawal action for about ten days as we kept moving westerly by north toward the Drina River and safety.

About two days from the Drina River by our calculation one of the Recon NCOs on the right of our position discovered forty emaciated disoriented Wehrmach soldiers in an isolated area who had been part of the rear guard of retreating soldiers who were the remnants of a Division that had escaped Belgrade by crossing the Sava River at Šabac . Many had marched west by north headed for safety in Visegrád. Their division had been virtually destroyed in vicious fighting in Belgrade by overwhelming Soviet forces with a large force of Tito's troops and Communist Partisans.

Our Recon man said they were relatively safe and he gave us

coordinates to send a detail with a medic and medical supplies and quarter rations of food. Large amounts of food probably would harm them until they got used to small portions. Their story was that they got separated in a snow storm and never could catch up. The Recon NCO also requested boots and socks, if any were available, as about half were barefoot or only had parts of boots left on their feet.

One of the lead Brigades sent a detail with supplies and a Medic, but no boots were available. Division was able to send some shoes officers had with their gear and socks.

Word was passed down about these men. It meant that the remnants of their Division were ahead of us or, with their headstart, probably already in Sarajevo.

The farther west we moved the smaller our enemy units who were trailing us, but rather than stand and fight, we had our men and so we kept pushing for the Drina River. We were able to cross the Drina River just North of Visegrád. It was after midnight on Christmas Day. As we approached an area outside of town to set up a temporary camp, we could hear Christmas music and cheerful sounds coming from the town. Headquarters had arrived much earlier and had a town doctor and nurses waiting with medical supplies to treat all the seriously wounded men immediately. Men with frostbite on their feet would be seen later in the day. Many lost toes and fingers but were saved from gangrene with this Godsend medical care. With adequate perimeter guards just in case, the rest of us enjoyed hot meals and showers in a small hotel. We repaired our clothing with supplies from the people of Visegrád and put cardboard or leather pieces in what remained of our boots. After cleaning and repairing all functioning weapons, we tried to relax with a few days of rest while Headquarters, which was far ahead of us, communicated with Sarajevo for new orders.

During this lull, Oberleutnant (First Lieutenant) Noack in this relaxed atmosphere made a critical error. He told a young Battalion Major that seeing all the men without adequate footwear and winter gear, that "maybe the war was lost." The Major stood him at attention and said he could have him shot for defeatism. Noack, at attention, assured him that he was a loyal officer with combat in

World War I and now. He would fight on no matter what. The seated young Major smiled and said, "Good, I'm waiting for orders for a new mission I will give to you." Oberleutnant Noack, still at attention, responded, "It would be an honor to accept this mission, sir." The Major replied, "Dismissed; go back to your unit as we start moving to Sarajevo in a few days. When I get the orders, I will call for you." Noack saluted with the Nazi party salute, and made sure to say Heil Hitler to his young, senior officer as he turned and left.

After moving toward Sarajevo for over a week, Noack felt that the mission must have been canceled. Several hours later he learned it was not canceled. The Division received new orders and he was told to report to the Major at Battalion Headquarters.

The Major seemed to be less stressed and greeted him civilly. He stated, "The Division has orders to send all wounded back to Sarajevo, but the Division will proceed with all speed below Sarajevo where the Drina River turns back into enemy territory. There is a pocket of Wehrmacht soldiers trapped inside their territory. The 22nd Division will rescue them and return to Sarajevo but,

Oberleutnant Noack, that is not your assignment. You are being given a new detachment for a critical mission. It will enhance all units at Sarajevo chances of being able to fight a withdrawal action toward Austria."

He continued, "In the morning you will be introduced to your new detachment, which is a highly trained Demo Team with Recon NCOs and a medic. You will be issued the weapons you request after you and your demo team plan the mission and your supply requirements. Get some rest tonight as you will need it. Report to me at 0700." Again, Oberleutnant Noack saluted and exclaimed, "Heil Hitler," and departed to rest.

Rising early, he reported to the Major at 0700 hours precisely. He was allowed to sit at a portable table with the Major as the men arrived and were introduced to their detachment commander. The Major had each man introduce himself and describe his specialty. Oberleutnant Noack was surprised to learn that one of them was a volunteer. He was one of the men who had escaped from Belgrade earlier in October, 1944. After the introductions and specialties were explained, the Major handed Noack an order to Division supply that Oberleutnant Noack was to be issued all equipment, supplies, and weapons they requested by 1600 hours on that date. The Major then read their orders aloud to all: "You are ordered to return to Yugoslavia on foot, avoiding all contact with the enemy and civilians to the best of your ability. Proceed to the area north of Visegrád, cross the Drina, and move at night toward Šabac on the Sava River. Destroy the traffic bridge crossing the Sava. This will slow down enemy troops trying to catch up to us as we retreat toward Austria. After you blow up the bridge, return to Sarajevo, and report to me. Understood?"

"Ja'wohl, Herr Major," answered Oberleutnant Noack.

The Major responded, "Take command, Herr Oberleutnant." He rose and walked out, leaving the tent to Noack and his men.

Noack's first task was to select his second in command in case he was killed. He was pleased to learn that one of the two Demo Specialists was a Master/Sergeant (Staubsfeldwebel) and was the highest ranking NCO. He naturally would be next in command.

Next in line was the other Demo Specialist, who was a Tech Sergeant (Oberfeldwebel), then one Sergeant (Unteroffizier), one Corporal (Obergefreiter), three Private First Class soldiers (Gefreiter) and one Private (Grenadier/Schutze).

Noack ordered his second in command to take the men to their tent and have them inspect, repair, and clean all weapons already in their possession and then start discarding items not necessary for survival. They were instructed to put all personal items that were important to them in one pile in their tent. He would get a lock and a footlocker. It would be left with the Supply Officer until their return. He put his Oberfeldwebel in charge while he and his Stabsfeldwebel reported to the central Supply and Weapons Center, which had been set up on arrival. He handed his orders with his list of supplies needed, rations, ammo, additional weapons, and white waterproof camo clothing with hoods, white helmet covers which could not be seen well when snowing. The explosives would be packed securely in two packs while wires, timers, and detonator would be packed in a third pack. Ammo pouches would be in two packs with rations for two weeks, and a small sled for additional ammo and needed tools, and rope. Explosives would be with the two Demo men at all times. Also, three machine pistols were ordered for the three ranking men. Others had their rifles and Noack and his two Senior NCOs were given sidearms (Walther P38's). The sled would also contain two Panzerfausts.

The supply officer told them they had been briefed and would do his best to have everything ready for pick up by 1600 hours as ordered by the Major. Oberleutnant Noack agreed to have his men back at 1600 hours, and he and his second in command departed. Returning to the tent where his men were cleaning and checking weapons, he told them to be at his tent at 1530 hours. He and his Stabsfeldwebel went to his quarters and started studying maps and brainstorming.

As Noack saw it, they had two advantages. First, the enemy knew that the 22nd Division had crossed into Visegrád at Christmas and probably thought they were in Sarajevo or on the way to Austria by now. They sure as hell were not expecting an attack and would be lax; especially the Communist partisans. Second, having one man who had crossed the bridge at Šabac in his escape from Belgrade would be valuable in terms of information on the construction and area terrain. Noack stated, "You and I need to talk with this man when we are not moving." His Senior NCO agreed. Next, he wanted his Senior NCO's opinion about rations, stating "Starting after breakfast when we move out at 0630 hours, I think since we are only getting two weeks of rations we need to go on half rations in case we get delayed going or returning. Who knows? What do you think?" Stabsfeldwebel Steiner agreed.

"Gút. Go back and take charge of our detachment and bring them here at 1530 hours." Steiner saluted and left.

Noack returned to the maps and thought "once we get out of range of sight and sound from the rear guard of the 22nd Division, we will be on our own." The safety of his men and the success of the mission was solely his responsibility, not the Major's. Therefore, they would not only bypass Visegrád during the night; they would cross over just above Visegrád out of sight and hearing and proceed toward Šabac on the west side of the Sava River far enough from roads to be barely visible in their white camo with the white background from snow. They would be ever harder to be seen at night as there would be no fires or stoves burning.

Knowing the area was mainly agricultural and that it was February, even daytime agricultural activity would be light. At most duties would be restricted to farm animal care and taking wood in for the fireplaces. With the enemy not expecting an attack and wintertime work routines made the mission not only a possible success but a probable success, he thought, "if we maintain discipline and plan each move carefully."

Before sun rise each morning when we would be seeking shelter where our white camo uniform covers would practically make us invisible, the Senior NCO would make sure, especially if not snowing, that one of the Privates would use the light rake on the sled to erase our footprints in the snow, mud, or ground for the last quarter kilometer. Also, the group, except for the forward Recon man, would walk side by side and step into the footprints of the man in ahead of him or single file in narrow places. This would make it easier to erase our trail whenever necessary, especially when preparing to hide and rest during the day.

Noack's thoughts and planning were interrupted by Steiner, his Senior NCO. It was now 1530. The men waited outside while Senior NCO Steiner entered the Commander's tent. Oberleutnant Noack told Steiner to go to Supply and take all supplies to the men's quarters and post an armed guard inside with the supplies and place a quarantined sign on the tent entrance. He was instructed to bring the guard's supper to him and to the Junior NCO who will stay with him and to do the same at 0530 hours when a large hot breakfast will be awaiting them. He told Steiner, "I will eat at 0500 and be ready to start the march toward Visegrád at 0630. Have all men and supplies ready by 0620 hours. Understood?"

Steiner snapped to attention and responded, "Ja'wohl, Herr Oberleutnant."

Noack smiled and said, "Go and pick up all supplies, equipment, weapons, rations, explosives, et cetera, take to the men's quarters, and get it all organized for our departure at 0630. After you are satisfied that they all know what they are doing and their duties on this mission, stop by and bring me up to date. Enjoy supper."

Steiner saluted, smiled, and walked out of the tent. He called the detachment to attention and marched them to the Supply Center. He inspected what he signed for and had it taken bit by bit to their quarantined tent, which the guard and NCO had posted. The balance of supplies were to be delivered to the tent and organized for the morning departure as it came in all prior to 0500 hours.

Later that night Steiner stopped by and informed his Commander that all would be in order by 0620 hours. He also reported that some special items may not be in until 0500 hours but would be issued to the medic or stored on the sled with the other equipment. Oberleutnant Noack realized that the 22nd Division could and would be resupplied as they marched past Sarajevo enroute to free another trapped unit. This unit was southeast of Sarajevo near where the Drina River meanders into friendly territory below Sarajevo. He had asked the young Major for some unusual but much needed items to be delivered before they departed. This must be the special items arriving as late as 0500 hours. Noack had asked for a supply of cough medicine with strong cough suppressants and extra socks for the nine men. The squad's silence was essential for this mission; a cough would give away their position. Fresh socks were needed to keep their feet healthy for quick movement when necessary. He also requested a month's supply of chewing tobacco as he was not allowing smoking once back into Yugoslavia. Also, he had asked that the Division Abwehr (Intelligence) send him a weather forecast for the month of February 1944 for Šabac , including the ice conditions on the Sava (Sau) River at Šabac . The Major had seemed surprised as he realized that he would not have thought of these things himself and thought, "Excellent. I have chosen the right man for the mission."

The Major had departed to put in his request for special items.

Another good sign was that Ernst Steiner, his second in command, had told him he had a close friend in Division Supply that owed him a big favor and he felt confident that we will have everything ready before 0600 hours. Marking a tent quarantined was a trick that Noack had learned in France to keep "dog robbing" of supplies to a minimum.

As Noack was about to lie down in his tent for some needed sleep, a courier asked permission to enter and, when granted, he stepped inside at attention without any verbal comment and saluted. When returned, he said, "Sir, I have a sealed envelope for you." Noack took the envelope, opened it, and saw that it was the weather report for February in the Šabac region. He thanked and dismissed the courier. If Steiner was right about the equipment and supplies, they had everything needed to accomplish the mission.

Before laying down again, he studied the brief weather report and was pleased. He poured himself a large double shot of Kognak and thought about the weather report: little sunshine, dark gray days, light drizzle or snow usual, and the Sava probably can't freeze over in Šabac as temperatures will hover between thirty and thirty-two degrees Fahrenheit at night and rise into the low forties by afternoon and then the temperatures will begin to fall down again. Perfect, he thought. I will share this with Stabsfeldwebel Steiner but no one else. Finishing his Kognak, he burned the weather report. He slept until 0430 hours. Arising, he brushed his teeth, shaved, and dressed in field gear, checked his sidearm, a Walther 9 mm P38, and left a stuffed pack on his cot while he went to breakfast at 0500 hours.

Due to the early hour, only the cooks were there just getting started, so he sipped on coffee while they prepared his last hot meal for a while. While sipping coffee, he thought, no need to break out the white camo until we enter enemy territory if snowing then. He also decided to have Steiner issue the machine pistol ordered for him to Unteroffizier Otto Schroeder with the two remaining ones going to Steiner and Oberfeldwebel Rudolf Graf. Schroeder's rifle would be stored on the sled. Orders to Steiner at 0600 hours before their formation at 0615 hours would be to put Unteroffizier Schroeder in charge of the rear on the march with three of the enlisted men (two PFCs and one private). They would have the duty of using a shovel and rake to erase our path for at least a quarter mile before entering our daytime hiding place when we reach enemy territory. All movement in Yugoslavia will be at night. The PFCs, private, and Sergeant Schroeder will keep watching our rear and right and left in order to avoid contact with individuals or groups or the enemy coming up on our rear. Schroeder will have one of the binoculars to scan both sides and the rear area. He will also check our trail to make sure no one dropped any trash; all paper and other disposable items will be buried at our campsite in the slit trench for urine and feces. When we leave, it will be covered with brush to hide the disturbed earth. A single piece of paper could give away our position and direction of travel. Rigorous discipline and constant observations of our surroundings will be needed.

His breakfast came with more coffee; he ate and thanked the cooks, departing to find Steiner, who had left Oberfeldwebel Graf in charge of getting them ready for their formation at 0615 hours. Their departure would be at 0630 hours moving north as the 22nd Division moved south. He and Stabsfeldwebel Steiner went to his tent where he picked up his gear while briefing Steiner on the instructions for their march and entry into Yugoslavia north of Visegrád at night. It would take two trips in their small raft.

He told Steiner, "Since the Drina flows north, they would start from their shore south of the landing area with all restrictions in force: No smoking, no discarding trash, no talking except for orders in a low voice, and use of hand signals when possible."

Since there was a possibility of the enemy crossing the Drina toward us, he expected everyone to be locked and loaded at all times, even on our side of the Drina. Corporal Fritz Peiper will be the Senior Recon man with PFC Max Berger the Junior Recon man, Berger staying with the rear guard unless Peiper needs him. Unterofficer Schroeder will be in charge of the rear guard. I will brief him later today when we take a break. The enlisted men can pull the sled and, if needed, this includes the cross-trained medic.

Noack told Steiner, "If you and Graf can secure the explosives safely on the sled until needed, that's fine, but check it frequently. We can't have any mistakes or senseless tragedies." Steiner responded, "Ja'wohl, Herr Oberleutnant." They left together for the formation.

On the way to the 0615 formation Oberleutnant Noack told Ernst to have Oberfeldwebel Graf (Rudy) to be ready to put everyone in a column of twos headed north, Senior Recon man, Corporal Fritz Peiper taking the point about one hundred yards out front and UnterOffizier Schroeder (Otto) and one of the PFCs (Gefreiters) and the one private (Grenadier/Schutze) in the rear with the sled. Getting close to the group, Noack told Ernst, "I will end my remarks at 0625 and walk around the group checking sidearms, machine pistols, and rifles; if there is no sign of the Major at 0630, I will nod; call them to attention and move them out north at exactly 0630. Make sure earlier to send the point man out about 0627. Tell the Grenadiers to move as quickly as possible with the sled determining the pace. Thank God it snowed last night; it should ease the sled's movement for the men."

Steiner responded, "Ja'wohl, Herr Oberleutnant."

Like clockwork, at 0627 Fritz Peiper started north as point man with instructions to follow on the route north the Division had used coming south. Noack thought Peiper must come back into sight and stop them if he saw anyone in their path. Noack told Steiner to brief Peiper on their first break.

On a cold snow falling day Noack hoped that they would not run into any friendlies. If they did, they would say they were on a training exercise and just about ready to turn back.

Of course, if enemy soldiers had crossed the Drina on their right, there would be a fight, but if we can, we will attempt to withdraw in a westerly direction deeper into friendly territory.

As the group headed north, after the first break, Fritz did not appear so they kept going. Soon the images behind them faded in the poor visibility. After about two hours, he had Ernst send the Junior Recon man PFC (Gefreiter) Max Berger forward to tell Fritz to take a thirty minute break while the group did the same.

After the break, Fritz, the Senior Recon man, would return to the group to debrief Ernst and the Commander and Max would take the next two hours guiding them around individuals or houses. The little group moved forward toward Visegrád. By any Army standards the group was top heavy with NCOs, four, and only four below NCO rank. This was necessary because all four had specialties needed to complete the mission. Two demo experts, Ernst, who also spoke Russian, and Rudy, who spoke Czech, would be handy in case they ran into civilians when they would be in civilian clothes walking near the bridge. Unteroffizier Otto Schroeder was an expert with Panzerfausts and grenades and would keep the group supplied from the sled and be their eyes and ears from the rear. Corporal (Obergefreiter) Fritz Peiper was an experienced Recon specialist who had recently been reduced in rank from an Unteroffizier. A company level disciplinary action had been taken stemming from a minor infraction; however, his combat record was excellent. Then there were the three PFCs (Gefreiters); one was cross-trained as an infantryman/ medic, and one private. The non medics were all infantrymen with expert rankings with their weapons. All had brief but deadly combat experience in the multiple engagements, rescuing fellow soldiers surrounded in Yugoslavia. They all knew what might lie ahead. They fully understood that their Commander was no paper-pushing Officer; Ernst had clued them in that Noack had seen combat in World War I and this time in Poland and France. He was with them in another unit as a company commander after the Hauptmann had been killed in Yugoslavia. Ernst Steiner had made it clear that they had one chance of being successful on their mission and getting back to Sarajevo: that was to follow all his orders to the letter. Then he explained to them that the Division had only given them two weeks of rations and that Oberleutnant Noack had decided, and he agreed wholeheartedly, that we must make it last a month. There will be times when we have to hold up for days to avoid Partisans and Tito's soldiers who will be close or for weather reasons. Therefore, as of today, we will all be on half rations, including our Commander, who is old enough to be your father. Grumbling, which is normal from the lower ranks, was at a minimum as Ernst had explained that it's better to have some food each day than none for two weeks if delayed. Unfortunately, surely to God, we probably will be behind schedule.

As Fritz Peiper was finishing his second turn at the Point, he found an ideal location about fifty yards off the trail down into a gulley where they would be out of sight if the weather cleared. Oberleutnant Noack and Stabsfeldwebel Ernst Steiner went to inspect and agreed. PFC Karl Schwarz and Private Wilhelm Thomsen dug a small trench for their latrine and trash disposal. Rudy Graf had the others setting up a lean-to and places for shelter halves and sleeping bags covered with ponchos. There would be no fires or smoking at night; chewing tobacco was available. Spit in the trench. As all of this was taking place as quietly as possible, Rudy Graf worked on the guard duty roster: two armed guards always on duty, both using two of the machine pistols. These weapons were automatic fire so you are able to fire in short bursts when feasible. Each would have extra ammo ready. Guards would be replaced every two hours through the night, one at each end of the small sleeping area. No talking. No breaks. Keep alert. Guard duty is only second to combat in terms of honor. At the morning formation Noack had opined about guard duty, "Your fellow soldiers are defenseless unless you protect and wake them." They could stand at ease but no sitting or leaning on a tree; Noack had also said, "Stand your tour and then rest easy as others protect you." They fully understood and performed their sacred duty well.

As Graf handed out the schedule by word of mouth and made sure each understood, Noack and Steiner walked far enough away to talk in low voices.

Noack stated, "Ernst, I think to get them ready for night marches into enemy territory we'd better switch to night marches about two days before we near Visegrád. What do you think?"

Ernst replied, "It makes good sense to me and I think we can work the problems out before we get to the spot on the Drina you selected to cross."

Noack nodded and they started back to the little camp. Noack suddenly stated, "One more thing, Ernst. Have Hans Mueller, the medic, report to me at the lean-to." Ernst, appearing surprised, asked, "Any problem I can help with?" Noack responded, "No, just want Hans to start inspecting everyone's feet tonight, including mine. Also, have Otto issue the medic nine small pieces of civilian cloth and one-half of a hand towel for nine every time we stop for that day."

Stabsfeldwebel responded, "Ja'wohl, Herr Oberleutnant."

Noack knew what he was doing and it was good for morale for them to see their Senior NCO following orders to the letter.

At the lean-to, Noack told Hans to sit down and began explaining to him the end of each day or at the beginning of each night the ritual they were starting. One at a time the men would come to the lean-to or whatever shelter they had and take their boots and socks off. Hans would inspect himself first and the Oberleutnant last. He would have a helmet full of water from melted snow or a small creek or wherever. Hans would give each man a clean piece of cloth and soap to wash his feet and rinse before Hans checked for blisters or other problems. Noack told Hans, "Our mission depends a lot on you. If someone can't move quickly when needed, we could all be killed or captured by the Communist partisans. That probably would be worse than death. Foot health is critical. Understand, Hans?"

Hans immediately rose, saluted, and said, "Ja'wohl, Herr Oberleutnant," to which Noack said, "Please sit and be at ease." He continued, "When you are done with a man, he is to wash his old socks and put on a fresh pair you will give him. Collect the dirty washcloths and towels when they finish, throw them in the slit trench to be covered and camouflaged before we move out. Tell each man that he is to take his wrung out socks and part of another hand towel and put between his poncho and sleeping bag. His body heat will dry the socks. They will rotate their two pair of socks until one needs to be replaced. When you need more washcloths, towels, or socks, just see Unteroffizier Schroeder at the sled. When socks are no longer useful, bury them in a slit trench." Noack advised young Hans to inspect himself after he gets all he needs to complete this important duty, then Noack stated, "I will have Stabsfeldwebel Steiner start sending the men before or after we eat half rations. Steiner will be next to last and will let me know when it is my turn."

Noack left the lean-to to inspect everything in the little camp. He also reminded Ernst to have Rudy check all weapons each night, especially the three machine pistols that will be used on Recon and guard duty, inspecting both before the first shift and after the last shift.

In the morning, after water and part of their half rations, he and Ernst checked the entire area including the latrine and made sure it was covered and hidden by pieces of brush over which they threw snow from a mound of snow about twenty feet away.

Before moving out, Oberleutnant Noack told Stabsfeldwebel Ernst Steiner to have Schroeder send Private Wilhelm Thomsen up to see him after we set up camp late this afternoon. Also, he instructed Ernst, "Order Fritz to look for animal trails to the left of human trails that run toward Visegrád and avoid human trails if possible. He is to brief his relief PFC Berger. They may as well get use to this before we cross the Drina. Move out our point man, Fritz, and in ten minutes move out the group." Steiner smiled and responded, "Ja, Herr Oberleutnant."

They moved out as ordered with Noack and Steiner up front. Ernst had mentioned earlier to the men that their Commander was a man who had worked his way up from a Grendier/Schutze. He not only was old enough to be their father, in fact, he could have been the grandfather of a few of them. This was good. The men liked him and were amazed at his stamina and were grateful for his accumulated experience and knowledge. Morale was good.

Going much slower using animal trails, they made their own path when trails turned the wrong direction until they found a new animal trail going north. Noack expected this slower pace in enemy territory. He wanted to get a realistic estimate of distance they could travel at night on animal trails to avoid all human contact. He also wanted his men to learn how to adapt to and master complications.

As they set up camp that evening, he estimated at their current pace it would be another three or four days until they passed Visegrád, which would be on their right about one-half mile or less. As Hans Mueller started the foot inspections, washings, and treatment, Noack found Steiner and Private Thomsen who had volunteered. He had crossed the bridge when escaping with the remnants of a Belgrade Division. His information would be highly useful for Ernst, the demo expert and second in command. He would need a cover story to explain why he was talking to Steiner and his Commander. He would let Steiner handle that.

After they moved away from camp, out of earshot, the three laid a poncho over a large log and sat down. It had been a colder, but clear day and they were adequately dressed. They were not in discomfort. Naturally Private Thomsen was tense in their presence. Noack told him to relax and speak freely; he was not in trouble. Noack went on, "We need your knowledge of the bridge in Šabac that you and your Division crossed when retreating from Belgrade. You can never speak to anyone about this except us. The reason for this is if any of us get captured the other six will not know what our mission is. This will make it safer for all of us." Thomsen understood and promised he would never tell anyone. He and Steiner got down to business with Ernst asking him all sorts of questions about the structure, the approach to it, and traffic flow. Thomsen said he had been a road guard for many hours at the bridge as parts of his Division crossed on foot. He said "It's only two lanes with a line down the center. Traffic was light, agriculture traffic and a few autos." He also reported that traffic dropped off a lot about 1930 hours to about one vehicle per hour. He advised, "There is one small guard shack at each end with one unarmed civilian guard. He stops traffic coming from his side if needed." Continuing, Thomsen said, "The guards are older, heavy set men who, after traffic slowed down, preferred to stoke up their coal stoves. They stayed in the shack, snacking on the food they brought from home and also snacked while lowering and raising the wooden barricade." He further stated he was relieved as road guard about 0200 hours on the east side of the bridge. He crossed to the west and then behind others marched northwest toward the Drina. His rear guard group got lost in a snow storm with high winds. He was one of the men found by the 22nd Division as they moved to the Drina and safety. He and the others were very grateful for being rescued.

Steiner was very happy with this information and asked, "Which side would be easiest to blow?"

Thomsen responded, "I don't know about easy, but it would take a lot longer to repair or replace if you took out the west side. All materials and equipment would have to cross the Sava (Sau) downriver near Belgrade."

Noack stood, smiled and said, "Wilhelm, that's very important information and it will help us succeed in our mission. God willing, we will get back in one piece."

Thomsen rose and stood at attention. He saluted and Noack returned it. Thomsen stated, "Thank you, sir. Please call me, Willie; I hate Wilheim," to which Noack responded, "Con mucho gusto." Steiner laughed and Willie looked puzzled. Noack explained to Willie, "My wife and I used to enjoy short vacations in Spain. Con mucho gusto means "with much pleasure." Thomsen laughed and said, "Thank you, sir." Noack said, "Ernst, you and Willie go ahead and work out his cover story on the way to the medic so your stories will be the same. I'm sure all six are curious. They do not need to know what we discussed for their own safety. You can tell them in Visegrád on the way back. Make sense?" Steiner answered, "Ja'wohl,

Herr Oberleutnant," and he and Willie started back working out their story. Noack followed about two minutes behind.

Fritz and Max had done a good job of finding animal trails headed in the right direction with short serpentine movements, but this was daytime. Noack was up first and went to each guard. They looked sharp. He complimented them. At dawn Noack went and tugged at Ernst's arm. He was up quickly asking, "Problem, sir?" Noack shook his head in a negative manner and motioned for him to follow him. About twenty feet away, he said, "Ernst, we have to find out how Fritz and Max do at night and at this pace we don't have much time for them to become as good at night as they were today in daylight, and this will slow us down more, but that's okay. I prefer to be late than dead." Steiner responded, "Agreed, sir."

Noack told Ernst to have Rudy Graf extend guard duty until 1800 hours, rations at 1715, break camp at 1800 hours, after you send Fritz out at 1750. Group moves out at 1800 hours. Noack continued, "Tell Graf to let me sleep in as much as possible and tell the medic to have each man air his boots out in the sun if not on guard. When men get up, have them check their weapons and have Graf inspect all weapons to see if they need a little oil. You and Graf alternate and get rest yourselves." Ernst responded, "Yes, sir."

After Ernst left, Oberleutnant Noack went to the medic, woke him, and took him on a short walk so as not to disturb the rest of the men. Noack talked to Hans in a soft friendly tone and explained that they were going on a night time schedule at 1700 hours and that all except those on guard duty should sleep in or rest until 1600 hours. His duties would start at 1600 hours. Noack ordered, "I want you to get nine sets of new socks from Sergeant Schroeder and enough powered milk for everyone. As you finish checking each man's feet, take his worst pair of socks, throw them in the slit trench, issue a new pair of socks and enough powered milk for an eight ounce canteen cup of milk to each one. I want each man to have some milk daily from this point on. Make sure to bury all trash in the slit trench. Between now and 1600 hours get all the rest you can. And one last thing, son, do what you can, what you were taught in basic training and again in advanced infantry and medic training about night vision. Explain to each man the procedure for night vision."

Hans Mueller replied, "Ja'wohl, Herr Oberleutnant."

Noack continued, "Good. Please tell each man, even the NCOs, as you check their feet to remember from this night on they must immediately close their best eye if a flare lights up or a searchlight is turned toward us. It is absolutely imperative that we all remain combat ready at all times. Our lives depend on it. It is just as easy for the Partisans to cross the Drina coming this way as it will be for us to enter their territory again. Understood, Hans?" "Ja'wohl, Herr Oberleutnant." Noack responded, "Gút. Go get some rest until 1600 hours."

Noack turned and went to his sleeping bag. He checked his sidearm for dirt and to see if it needed a little oil in this damp weather. He also made sure that his four spare clips were fully loaded with nine millimeter ammo. After this, he left things up to Ernst and Rudy, who were alternating being up with the rotating guards.

Upon arising at 1430 hours, Noack washed his hands and face. He had made shaving optional until they returned in case two or three escaped after an engagement. They would look more like a civilian if they were not clean shaven in the civilian clothes stored on the sled for escapes and recon work.

Schroeder had nine sets of civilian clothes in the sled. Besides the Commander, only Ernst and Rudy knew this. They had selected all civilian clothes, which may or may not be used, when they were ready to reconnoiter the bridge. They had the sizes of the other seven and had obtained an additional supply of boots, pants, shirts, jackets, and hats for all. These clothes were typical garb for Serbians and Yugoslavian Partisans and had been delivered by air on a Luftwaffe Junker cargo plane to Sarajevo; compliments of Abwehr. Sarajevo had sent them out to the 22nd Infantry supply and made available to Stabsfeldwebel Steiner and Feldwebel Rudolf Graf. They made selections for the mission after the Major had approved an eight man team plus their Commander.

After washing up, Noack found that Rudy was on duty and

Ernst was sleeping. He told Rudy, "Tell the two Recon men taking the point until we cross the Drina to look for and find a campsite off our route to the left about a quarter mile in a dense area by 0500 hours and send word back to a third man who will go forward to meet one of them and return to guide us. I need to talk to all men briefly after we get the camp set up and Guards posted. I will brief the guards individually." Rudy responded, "Ja'wohl, Herr Oberleutnant."

Before talking to the men, after their small camp was set up Noack took Ernst and Rudy for a short walk and expressed his concerns. He opined, "Our rate of movement has more than doubled in terms of slowness. At this rate we should be safe but slower than the good Major wanted. Mission is first, our safety second, but in my opinion it doesn't matter when we blow the bridge as long as we blow it. The Division will be waiting on us or some of us to return before they leave Sarajevo if they get back before us. Therefore, it is my decision to go with slowness and complete the mission when we get there. After the mission, we can drop a lot of gear other than rations and ammo and travel as fast as possible to safety in Visegrád." Both agreed on the decision to be safe first and then the mission could be completed. Ernst said, "We can worry about the Major's timetable when they return." The three headed back to the other men as the sun was up but not a lot of sunshine on a gray chilly day.

Noack spoke in a low voice to the six men who were sitting on their ponchos over the snow covered ground while Steiner and Rudy took guard. He started, "We don't know a lot about each other as we all came from different Battalions and Brigades, but I'm pleased to be with you. Each of you have carried out your assigned duties with skill and are excellent examples of the Wehrmacht Heer soldier. It is my honor to lead you and I will do my best to get us all back to our Division. We are moving at a slow but safe pace. I expect that barring the unexpected we will pass to the left of Visegrád about four or five nights from now. The night before we bypass Visegrád I want each of us to have two or three grenades with us at all times. I want Unteroffizier Schroeder to issue one

Panzerfaust to the person who has the most experience firing them.

I doubt if we will run into any T34s across the river but only God knows. We will be ready and we can use it against fixed positions if we can't go around it. I do expect that we will run into company size clusters of Partisans. Hopefully Fritz will be able to steer us away from them. There are now two sets of Partisans. One used to be our ally but changed sides about fourteen months ago, the Chetniks. They were loyal Royalists and hate the Communist group of Partisans. The Chetniks have bright uniforms and are the most disciplined. The Communists are sloppy and poorly disciplined as troops. They tend to have bright campfires at night and drink any alcohol they can steal. Once they get going it would be easy to attack and eliminate them, but that's not our mission. I hope they are loud enough to tip Fritz off so we can take a wide berth around them. The Chetniks won't be so easy. Some of you may have worked with them when they were our ally. Rest assured they are not our friends any more. About thirteen or fourteen months ago the Chetniks killed over three hundred of our fellow soldiers and wounded another four hundred or so in Visegrád when they crossed the Drina to destroy the railroad bridge. Over two thousand Chetniks, assisted by American and British advisors, raided the small Visegrád garrison and destroyed our unit there. Chetniks might look like toy soldiers, but I assure you they are well trained. With only nine of us we need to avoid them and the Communists. If they sneak across the area we are moving into, we must avoid contact even if we have to do an about face and march back to our previous camp. The mission will be there when we get there. We can get around the Communists once Fritz or Max spot them and then backtrack to us. If they think we can get around them, we will proceed around them after the campfires get going and the alcohol starts flowing. If we have no way around them and cannot backtrack, we will plan our attack for late that night after even their guards have relaxed and the rest are drunk. None of them are expecting an attack, especially not by a squad sized unit. Surprise will be our best weapon if we have to fight. But remember our mission is not to fight but to deliver Ernst and Rudy to Šabac. Then we are going to reconnoiter and then return to Sarajevo. That's all I have to say. Any questions?"

One NCO, Obergefreiter Fritz Peiper, raised his hand and asked, "Why did the Chetniks double-cross us and change sides, Herr Oberleutnant?"

Noack responded, "Good question. I've asked myself that same question a few times. I don't have any idea." Walking toward the guards to release them, Noack said, "Ernst, they're all yours."

After this, he returned to see if Hans was ready for his foot inspection. After waiting his turn and Hans had treated a small blister, he returned to his gear and slept until 1400 hours. Then they prepared to eat and close camp and move north again with Fritz and Max going out one at a time in front of the group, Oberleutnant Noack at the front and Schroeder and Private Willie Thomsen behind the sled. After they found a well-marked trail in the snow with two clear sets of footprints, Noack instructed Rudy to fall back and relieve Otto for a few minutes. He needed to talk with Otto. Rudy fell out and Otto ran forward, stating "You want me, Herr Oberleutnant?"

"Ja, Otto. Starting tonight and every night from now until the mission ends you must help Willie do a perfect job covering our tracks with the shovel and rake for the last quarter mile of our tracks until we reach a campsite before dawn. If you are not in camp with no trail to us within thirty minutes, I will have someone backtrack to assist you. Keep that machine pistol fully loaded and ready just in case. Do you have a preference on which other man, if needed?"

"Ja, Oberleutnant, I do with your permission."

"Of course," responded Noack.

"Sir, PFC Karl Schwartz was a construction worker before the war and would be very helpful."

"Thank you, Otto. That's very useful information. Whenever you're running late, I will have Karl backtrack to you. We are depending on you to make us disappear."

"Ja'wohl, Herr Oberleutnant. It will be done."

"Thank you, Unteroffizier Schroeder. Go ahead and ask Rudy to fall back in with Ernst." "Ja'wohl, Herr Oberleutnant."

He ran back, helped Willie get the sled up a small incline.

After this, Karl was always with the sled along with Willie, and Hans helped when not carrying out his medic duties.

It was a clear, cold night as they moved north, turning left and then back to the right whenever obstacles would block the sled in the rear. All nine men knew that the concept of cold was relative. They all had friends or relatives who served during "Unternehmen Barbarossa." Those who made it back reported a scene like Napoleon's men had encountered at the gates of Moscow in the winter of a prior century. Men who fell asleep froze to death. Wounded men who had no fellow soldiers nearby nearly froze when they fell. All nine men knew that this weather was a blessing and did not complain. Even half rations and plenty of water was a blessing.

The little group was making pretty good time this night and took short breaks about every hour. After one of the breaks at about 0200 hours, Hans Mueller, who usually stayed in the rear, heard a muffled groan from behind him in the sled. It was Karl Schwartz, who had stepped through the two to three inches of snow onto a board with a long nail protruding through it. Medic Hans Mueller told him to stand still and shift his weight to the other leg and then he ran up to Stabsfeldwebel Steiner and reported. Of course, Oberleutnant Noack could hear the report from the medic before Hans concluded. Noack halted the group and sent a runner north to stop the Recon men until notified to restart.

Hans and Unteroffizier Schroeder stepped onto the cleared off board while Karl pulled his foot off the nail, which had entered his right foot on the pad behind his toes. Hans cleaned the wound, put medication and a bandage on it with a fresh pair of socks for both feet.

Noack had watched and was pleased with Hans' work. He sent a runner to tell Fritz and Max to restart in thirty minutes, which would give Karl and all the rest a break.

After the Commander was back up front talking with Ernst and Rudy, Hans came forward to report that he was free if they needed anything. Noack asked about a tetanus shot and Hans told him that Karl had one less than a year ago, so he was in good shape. Noack said, "You did well, Hans. We are lucky to have you with us.

Go on back and tell everyone Karl is okay. We move out in forty-five minutes."

"Ja'wohl, Herr Oberleutnant," Hans replied, and saluted, not the party's salute but a soldier's salute. Noack returned it. Hans returned to the rear, telling everyone in a low voice Karl was fine. From that moment on, only the soldier's salute was used by all.

After the rest break, they slowly moved out. The temperature was about thirty-two degrees Fahrenheit, the night clear, so visibility was as good as the Recon men's eyesight. We were just following their footsteps and prepared to cover the trail the last quarter mile or so before setting up camp.

For the next three days they moved slowly north toward Visegrád without incident with temperatures in the thirties. During the day while camouflaged in the woods, the temperature hovered between the high thirties and low forties. On the third evening around 1700 hours while preparing to eat and close camp to travel north, it started to drizzle with mixed light snow.

By 0500 hours when they met Fritz and Max in the next

campsite, it was only drizzle. Noack thought, "Good. This will simulate the type of weather we will encounter all the way to Šabac, cold rain or snow or a mixture. Any civilian with common sense will stay indoors. The Communist Partisans will be hunkered down in their camps. This will give us a good test of our rate of travel and how the men were able to stay combat ready."

Everyone had performed well and they were getting close to Visegrád, so Oberleutnant Noack decided to have another talk with the two Recon men, Fritz and Max while they sat under two outstretched ponchos overhead and a third poncho on the ground. Noack told them to speak freely and be at ease.

Noack's facial hair had lots of gray and was much more pronounced then the two young men who were barely in their twenties, if that. Noack found his mind wandering back to his home, his wife, Johanna, son, Hans-Jürgen, now age ten, and his little daughter, Hannelore, who would be four in May 1945, just three months away.

He snapped back to the moment and addressed the men. "We

will need to keep a close watch for the first houses on the outskirts of Visegrád. Even though they are our allies, we cannot be seen by anyone or it could endanger the mission and get us all killed. These people do trade across the Drina River. Rumors of our presence will alert out enemy. Understand?" Both replied, "Ja'wohl, Herr Oberleutnant."

"Good. I want you to cut left sharply when you first see the outskirts, making sure that we will be out of sight as we are moving to the left. I will leave it to your judgment how far we go to the left, whether a quarter mile or a half mile, as long as you find a dense safe place for our day camp. It must not be visible to Visegrád's outskirts or any elevated positions or roads to Visegrád. If we have to cross a road to get to the camp site, the nearest Recon man will return to the ground and assist Unteroffizier Schroeder, Karl, and Willie as they cover the trail to and from the road so no motorist or hiker sees our trail to the road should they start wondering what is going on. Understood?" "Ja'wohl, Herr Oberleutnant."

"Good. See the medic, have some milk and a snack, and get

some sleep." They arose, turned around and saluted. He remained seated while returning the salute. He felt cold, wet, and too damned tired to get up. He knew Ernst and Rudy would handle things in a military manner while he dried off and got some much needed sleep.

The next thing he knew Ernst was waking him to get ready to close the camp and set out after dusk dark. They would head for Visegrád and then turn right for the amount of time they had gone to the left, hopefully coming out above Visegrád close to the Drina. They would pick a safe campsite about a twenty minute walk from the Drina.

After marching about an hour and a half, Max came running back to the group, telling Stabsfeldwebel Steiner that they were too close to the outskirts, turn back left sharply for twenty minutes and then back to the right until we found Fritz. Max said, "Follow me."

Max left only a few minutes before them so they could follow him easily. Noack thought, "By the time we get close to the Drina River at the campsite, dawn will be breaking." This concerned him and he was right. While Schroeder, Willie, and a slightly limping Karl erased their trail into the camp, the others got things covered up as the temperature started to drop in the dawning day's gray light.

After everything was in order and the men had some milk, had their foot inspection, and began to get into their sleeping bags as the guards were posted, Noack sent for Ernst, Rudy, and Otto, the three Senior NCOs. He told them to relax and speak freely at all times as they will be entering enemy territory tonight with a small team to check the landing sites for the group and reconnoiter toward Šabac for about an hour and then return. He advised them, "Senior Recon man Fritz had found a great spot where the Drina meanders into a small half circle and the distance from shore to shore is about seventy-five yards."

Oberleutnant Noack continued, "I think only one Recon man, one demo man, and one person to hide the raft and guard it covered by whatever is available until you return, then the three return here and report to me your findings. If all goes well and it is unpopulated, we will leave for Šabac and our mission tomorrow night. Now, let's agree on who will be the three who will go tonight."

Stabsfeldwebel Steiner spoke first stating, "Sir, as Senior NCO, it is my place to lead this team tonight. I think Corporal Fritz Peiper as Recon and PFC Schwartz. Fritz and I can see a lot in an hour. With your permission, sir, I will see Fritz in a few minutes and get his description of the crossing site and type of terrain close to shore to hide the raft."

Noack replied, "Permission granted. All right. Then Otto, go empty out the raft and paddles and make sure the three men have enough extra ammo in the raft if needed."

"Ja'wohl, Herr Oberleutnant," Otto replied, as he departed.

Then Noack smiled as they walked away a few feet and said, "Ernst, you get with Fritz and Karl and explain tonight's mission and then sleep until 1800 hours. Eat, check your canteens, weapons, and ammo. Also get Rudy to let Fritz have his machine pistol tonight and Karl his sidearm." Both looked into each other's eyes for a long few seconds knowing the shit was about to hit the fan.

Ernst replied, "Ja'wohl, Herr Oberleutnant," saluted, walking away as Noack stood and returned the salute, "I'll see you all before you leave for the Drina." Steiner turned, smiling at this brave old man, and nodded his head in a positive manner.

Noack arose at 1730 hours and got cleaned up, dressed, and through the dense woods walked over to eat his rations with Ernst. Ernst told his commander that Fritz said the landing area is desolate. There is a bend blocking the view from Visegrád and from the other direction, and plenty of brush for Karl to use hiding himself and the raft while he and Fritz explore the area going toward Šabac . Noack was happy and said, "Please give Fritz my compliments and I wish the three of you Godspeed." As it was getting time, Noack excused himself and went down to the raft to wish Fritz and Karl good luck. This done, he went back to his spot and sent for Rudy and Max for their briefing. They were saying goodbye to the men going out on the mission but arrived within three or four minutes. Noack told them to relax and be seated.

While Rudy got a chew of tobacco and Max declined an offer of a chew, Noack thought of what he would say. He had to make them understand but also know that the safety of Ernst, Fritz, and Karl was in his heart as well as theirs. He spoke slowly and softly to these two young soldiers with limited experience, saying "I pray that our three men will return safety by 2400 hours, but they may not. Our men and our enemy are in the hands of God. We have to plan for the worst and all pray for the best, and we must be ready to repel an attack if they get into a fight."

Continuing, he said, "As soon as we finish here, Rudy, I want you to pick up a third guard with the most combat experience and send him out at 2200 hours to a point about halfway between us and the Drina River. If he sees our men on the way, have him join them. If he hears gunshots or sees enemy movement, tell him to backtrack quietly halfway and then fire two quick shots from his sidearm and run the rest of the way back to us. We will be moving to our fallback position, which will be our former garrison in Visegrád. It will give us good cover in all directions. Also, the Mayor is loyal to us and may be able to hide us in plain sight. We will change into civilian clothing. If the guard misses us, he will see our trail to the garrison."

To Max, Noack said, "Go tell Otto and Willie to repack everything back onto the sled and point it to Visegrád." To Rudy he said, "You tell everyone to get all your gear ready and be fully dressed, locked and loaded with easy access to their grenades. If they hear two shots prior to our Recon team returning, it means we will double time back to Visegrád and the garrison with the sled being assisted by all. If our team gets back safely, you will unpack again, and I will brief you when Ernst finishes briefing me. We will then repost guards and get some rest."

"In the meantime," Noack said, "check all weapons carefully." He stated to Rudy and Max, "Go get it done."

The Oberleutnant could not rest. He paced in circles around their small encampment checking things as he went. Time lagged on.

After 0040 hours, Noack heard soft noise coming from the area of the perimeter guard nearest the direction the team had taken, so he walked in that direction. It was the team coming into camp. He silently said, "Thank you, Lord." He told Rudy to take charge of the other men while he met with the three returning men and trail guard.

The four huddled together under four ponchos laying on a cords. Noack broke out his last bottle of Kognak, which was about three-quarters full. He told them how proud of them he was and grateful to our Lord for getting them back safely. He handed them the bottle and said, "There is enough for each of us to have three shots while you're bringing me up to date."

Ernst started reporting their activity: "Sir, it went well. We will have no problem getting all nine of us and supplies in two trips. It is totally isolated for about three miles inland toward Šabac . Then we will have to have Fritz and Max find serpentine routes around this agricultural region, working our way toward the Sava which flows the way we are headed."

Ernst continued, "Since it is winter and the weather seems to alternate between snow and rain, the ground is a mess. Most farm families, except for early morning duties, will stay indoors. There are enough stretches of forests to find places to camouflage ourselves during the day. As long as we are very quiet early in the morning as they do their farm chores, we will be safe. We need to make camp before the sun comes up to camouflage ourselves, especially if we are close to someone's residence. We will be able to judge our distance from them by the sparks and smoke from their chimney. Sir, has Private Thomsen given you all the information he has about the terrain and bridge?" Noack thought for a second and responded, "Yes, I'm sure he has. He is a brave young man." Ernst smiled, agreeing, "I'm sure of that, sir. Since you think there is nothing else we can gain from him in terms of information, it is my opinion, sir, that this mission does not need him and all the equipment and supplies. Rudy and I can carry the explosives, wire, detonator, and our weapons. Someone else can carry the extra ammo and rations for five to seven days, which we will divide into half rations with the help from the medic and you, Oberleutnant, to lead us.

Willie can take the raft back across the Drina River. Otto and the men can take it back to our camp. Private Thomas will erase all signs of us with the rake before boarding the raft. When the equipment and men are in the woods on our side of the Drina,

Willie will erase the footprints across the shore up to the wooded trail."

Oberleutnant Noack stated, "Makes us lighter and faster, good thinking. Who are the others who you think will be most helpful for the mission and why?"

Ernst replied without thought or hesitation, "Corporal Fritz Peiper, Senior Recon man, and PFC Hans Mueller, medic. There is a higher probability that one or more of us may get wounded than anyone who remains across the Drina."

"Well taken, Ernst," stated Noack. He then looked at NCO Corporal Fritz Peiper and said, "Fritz, not a word to anyone, but go tell Sergeant Schroeder to report to me now. You stay with the sled and supplies until he returns."

Fritz stood, saluted, and said "Ja'wohl, Herr Oberleutnant," and left.

When Sergeant Otto Schroeder arrived, Noack told him to sit and offered him a shot of Kognak, which was all that was left in the bottle. Noack began to explain that the group was being divided to enhance speed and increase the probability of mission success. Everyone would go to the Drina crossing tonight. However, he said, "You, the raft, and the rest of the men will return to this camp and wait for us for fifteen days. We will fire off a flare which we will bury tonight for further use on the other side of the Drina. When you see that flare, you and two men bring that raft as fast as possible and be ready to leave for Visegrád as soon as we get across and move out. The flare may be early or late, but when you see it, come get us. If we are not back by the fifteenth night, go to the old garrison at Visegrád. Set up camp for another four days. If we aren't back by then, head to Sarajevo for supplies and new orders. Questions, Otto?" Otto responded by saying, "no, sir."

Noack said, "Good. Otto, before we leave, bring me a Panzerfaust just in case. I will carry it. Peiper will get my machine pistol. This should give us plenty of firepower with three MP40s. Make sure Fritz, Ernst, and Rudy have plenty of ammo and grenades."

Sergeant Schroeder looked disappointed that he would not be

going on the final leg of the mission but understood the need for speed with a lighter load. He was standing at attention when he saluted smartly and, full of emotion, said, "My God in heaven, sir. I wish you all God's protection and wish I could be with you." Oberleutnant Noack stood erectly and, returning the salute, said, "Thank you, Otto. You have done a fine job. Take command of your group and be ready to take us to cross the Drina by 1900 hours. I will send you the word when we are ready. Dismissed."

After Otto departed, Noack told Ernst to get his group packed up with everything they would need and to tell Otto I want all of us to get full rations tonight about 1700 hours. He ordered, "At 1800 hours the two groups will meet separately with you and Otto double checking that we have everything required to get to and blow that damned bridge in Šabac ." Ernst understood, and Noack said, "I'm going to get some sleep, Ernst, I'll see you at 1700 hours."

That afternoon about 1650 hours, Otto was close to Noack's sleeping bag. Hearing him, Noack raised up.

"Sir, I'm sorry to disturb you."

Noack said, "No problem. What's the situation?"

"Sir, all is moving smoothly. I just brought your Panzerfaust so you could look it over, sir."

"Good idea. Thanks."

Otto saluted and returned to the sled and his men. Noack raised his hand in a sleepy salute. After he washed up, he sent for Max Berger, who was in Otto's group. Max was the other Recon man but more importantly he was an expert on Panzerfausts. Noack hadn't handled one since 1939 at the Retraining Center in Berlin. He had seen his men to use them in Poland and France, but he hadn't fired one. Berger went about half an hour getting him checked out on the Panzerfaust, which was similar to the Allies' bazooka. Noack then handed Berger his machine pistol which Fritz had returned last night. Noack told Max, "Thanks for a very needed session on the Panzerfaust. Please take my machine pistol to Fritz. Help him check every part, clean, oil, and dry fire it. Issue him as much ammo as he can carry. Also tell Hans in addition to medical supplies he needs to carry some extra ammo. I will also because the two Demo men are fully loaded and can't carry any more weight. Hans and I will have to keep the three with machine pistols resupplied with ammo when needed if we get into a fight. Questions?"

"No, sir."

Max took the machine pistol and slung it on his left shoulder, stood at attention and saluted, saying "Ja'wohl, Herr Oberleutnant." He left and Noack went to eat with Ernst and to see things for himself. Later he met at the sled with Otto and Ernst, who advised that all was in order. He decided to sit and write a letter to Johanna and his children in case he didn't make it back. After sealing it, he took it to Otto and asked him to mail it from Visegrád on the nineteenth day if they had not returned. He then turned his mind one hundred percent to his task at hand, the mission: blow the bridge at Šabac .

Returning to the sled, he told Unteroffizier Otto Schroeder, "About 1830 we will inspect all five packs, rope, and flare gun for our return. Have the men not on the bridge mission carry the packs and supplies to the shore of the Drina with the raft. This will give us a little edge when we move out on the other side. Also remember you and Willie will need the rake, shovel, and flashlight to erase our footprints and anything dropped on both shores. You will have lots of time if Fritz is right, and I think he is."

Otto answered, "Ja'wohl. It will be done, sir."

The drizzle had stopped about 1300 hours, but it was still an overcast, chilly, gloomy evening as Noack got ready. As he finished inspecting packs and the raft with Ernst, Hans appeared and said, "Sorry, sir, but I thought I would see you before we leave." Noack laughed and retorted, "Damn, Hans, I think you can read my mind," to which he responded, "No, sir, I just know your feet are a little older than ours and may need more care." Noack thanked Hans and sat back. After looking at his Commander's feet, Hans said, "Sir, you have a small corn on the left little toe that will start rubbing against your boot. I'm putting a small plaster over it. If it gets to be a problem for you, let me know. I am cutting a small hole in your left boot so it won't rub. You can wear a double sock on your left foot if you like." Hans stood, started to salute, and Noack waved him off, saying, "Have you checked all the men?"

"Yes, sir."

Noack replied, "Good job, Hans." Hans looked directly into his eyes like a son to his father and said, "Thank you, sir."

After lacing up his boots, Noack was aware of the corn plaster, but since it felt better than without it, he left to make a final check on things. He told Otto that the perimeter guard going out toward the Drina should get out there quickly One man not on the bridge mission ate early and was used to relieve all three guards, one at a time. Otto responded at attention as the others were near. "Ja'wohl, Oberleutnant," as he saluted. Noack stood erect and returned his salute, stating, "Otto, remember the story I told you about Alsace. Keep your perimeter guard sharp." Otto replied, "Ja'wohl, Herr Oberleutnant. Thank you, sir."

Noack headed back to the raft. As he rechecked the five packs, flare gun, weapons, explosives, rope, and ammo pouches for each man, Fritz asked his Commander if he could tell Otto about the shore area. Noack responded, "Of course, Corporal, speak freely."

"Thank you, sir."

Fritz then told Otto that he had placed a rock at the spot where the raft will enter the Drina. "We will then be paddling with the current, making it quicker to reach the middle of the half circle land formation that hides us from sight. After you erase our footprints on the enemy shore as you head back, you will be paddling against the current all the way. It will be difficult to land close to the rock. It will be easier to erase our footprints if you can land as close to our departure trail as you can."

Noack broke in as he and Steiner rose to go and said, "Otto, that's good advice as you must erase every trace of all of us on both shores if it takes you all night. We cannot afford to be spotted."

Otto stood at attention saying, "Sir, I assure you it will be done, Godspeed to all of you," as he turned and left for the raft just ahead of his Commander and the Senior NCO.

About 1855 hours after each of the five had their turn at the slit trench and washed their hands, they saw the raft and men with their packs and other items waiting on the trail to the Drina. Noack told Fritz to take point and lead Otto and the raft to the rock on the shore so they would put the raft in at the correct spot. Fritz saluted and left quickly. Noack and the bridge mission men followed behind the raft single file.

They arrived at the trail opening to the river about 1930. No rain since earlier in the day, still overcast with poor visibility and the temperature was dropping slightly to a chilly thirty-five degrees Fahrenheit as they pushed off in the raft. Fritz was right; the current grabbed them moving toward the Sava. All they really had to do was make slight corrections with paddling to steer. They landed dead center in the middle of the half-circle cove that blocked views from Visegrád and from the area where the Drina eventually flows into the Sava. The Sava flowed down from the confluence of two streams in the Julian Alps downhill all the way in a southeasterly direction until reaching Belgrade, at which point it joins the Danube. It empties into the Black Sea through Romania.

They got the raft up far enough not to drift out. Noack asked

Fritz to get a shovel and show him where he should bury the flare gun now stored in a waterproof canister. After Fritz finished burying it, he put dead brush over the sandy soil. They walked back to the raft. After talking with Otto about maintaining strict control so they would be safe, he returned to the raft and put on his pack full of rations. He also had an extra machine pistol and ammo. He slung the Panzerfaust over his left shoulder and the MP over his right shoulder.

Ernst came up and said, "Sir, all is in order. What are your orders?"

Noack responded, "Good, Ernst. Send Fritz forward after we finish. We will follow single file in his footsteps in six minutes. You will be the point and Rudy will be the rear guard. Machine pistols front and back. Tell Fritz if he sees Partisans, Communists or Chetniks or their camps to backtrack to us as fast as possible so we can decide which direction to go to avoid all contact."

"Yes, sir, I will brief him and send him out now."

Noack, Rudy, and Hans watched from their cover as Willie

and Otto erased the last signs of their arrival, hopped into the raft while in ankle deep water, and started paddling immediately as the current tried to pull them toward the Sava. Both paddled like a precision team, and they eventually landed fifteen to twenty feet from the rock. Joining the two that remained on the far shore, they walked in the water dragging the raft down to the rock and reentered the trail to the woods. Of course, Noack, Rudy, and Hans did not see this but knew that they made it as they heard no noise, gunshots, or voices.

The demo team waited just about where the flare gun was buried for Ernst to return and lead them out toward Šabac about seven to ten minutes behind the Senior Recon man, Corporal Fritz Peiper. The other four knew their lives were in his hands but were highly confident in his recon skills. Ernst was there in the dark and whispered, "Follow me, sir." Noack followed in Steiner's footprints as Hans followed the Commander and Rudy trailed behind them, keeping an eye on the rear and both sides of their trail looking for campfires or people or enemy troops, each of which would be bad news. Steiner also watched the forward area for a fast Fritz backtracking to give adequate notice for fight or flight. More than likely it would be flight if they had a choice. Steiner didn't know but felt that his Commander was going to carry out the order to blow the bridge at Šabac no matter what. We were going to help protect retreating fellow Wehrmach Heer soldiers and some Waffen SS disposition soldiers escape!

The Waffen SS had many wounded and killed while helping Heer troops. They were young, well trained, elite troops and the Heer had welcomed their support. Noack had privately shared his opinion with Senior NCO Ernst Steiner that it was a shame that the political SS worked under the SD in Berlin. They handled black operations, political assassinations, and any crazy thing ordered from the top. They were not trained soldiers. They should have been given another name like the allied counterparts or the Waffen SS disposition troops should have been renamed. Noack was concerned that German citizens after the war, as most citizens in most countries don't know shit about the military, would confuse the fine combat soldiers who fought with distinction alongside us many times with the Political SS. This is not true. Noack felt strongly that the Political SS were not part of the military and were not fit to carry the jock straps of Heer or Waffen SS disposition soldiers. He said, "Some of the Political SS were criminals before the war and most during the war."

Ernst knew that World War I and World War II experiences gave Noack a more in depth understanding of what was going on outside of their theatre of operation. Ernst, knowing the danger to this loyal German officer, repeated and reported nothing.

Ernst knew with only five men Noack would not start a fight unless they were fired on and if it was their only choice. Their mission was to blow the bridge, not to win running gun battles as we had done racing through Yugoslavia creating corridors for our trapped troops.

The five walked on into the night. A few snowflakes fell, but it was all mud on the ground. The temperature by 0300 hours was down to thirty degrees Fahrenheit. At about 0130 Fritz had come back to the column point, Stabsfeldwebel Steiner, and told him that he had found a nice wooded area that would be safe in the daytime.

While they made camp, he would go back out and find the route for the next night. Steiner told him to sit and rest; he would go back and ask the Commander. Noack told Rudy and Hans to "take ten" while he talked to Ernst. Ernst briefed Noack and he thought it was a good plan. Ernst headed back and told Fritz, "approved with a big smile." Fritz smiled, too, and headed back on his path to the camp site. Steiner sat on his poncho until the three arrived. They joined Steiner on their ponchos for another ten minutes and then arose, folding their ponchos after brushing off the mud. Then the three followed behind Pointman Ernst Steiner. By 0430 they met up with Fritz and set up their small camp with the same procedures but only one guard with a machine pistol always on duty and rotated every two hours between Steiner, Graf, and Mueller.

The password was one bird call and the guard would know Fritz was back after having been out. Any problems, Fritz would backtrack to the camp and the Commander would decide our course of action.

Fritz approached the camp just at sunup and used his bird call once and slowly approached the perimeter guard. After Ernst, who was arising to relieve Hans on guard duty, saw Fritz taking off his gear; he told him to get some milk and crackers. He could relax until Ernst returned with Oberleutnant Noack. Ernst moved quietly as the sunlight was making the forest visible. The sounds of nature were starting. After a stiff, middle-aged Noack was up and had washed his hands and face, Ernst told him that Fritz was just back and getting ready to sleep. Noack said, "Good news, indeed. Let's go get briefed." As they neared Fritz, he started to rise to report to Noack, but his Commander waved for him to remain seated. Noack sat close to Fritz on his right and Ernst returned to his guard post. Noack spoke in a low tone to Fritz. "Give me the good news first." Fritz smiled and started, "Sir, it's mostly good. I made it, by my best estimate, six more miles nearer the bridge. I estimate we will need, depending on the weather, five or six more night marches to be in striking distance. Then it will depend on how much time the demo team needs to reconnoiter the bridge at Šabac . The bad news, sir, is that we need to go out an hour or more later and make camp an hour sooner. That's two to three hours less of our marching time daily, which will add an extra day or two before we arrive close to the bridge."

Noack stated in a military manner, "Excellent report, Corporal Peiper. Tell us why do we need to lose two to three hours per day?"

Fritz responded, "Sir, from this point on we need to stay in the dark at all times, coming in to a hiding place an hour or more before dawn and not going out until most people have eaten and gone to bed. We will be passing through an agricultural area with little clusters of farm houses, barns, and streams. There are stands of trees all along the Sava Basin that we can be camouflaged in during pre-dawn hours, but it is too risky not to be invisible whenever there is light. Probably the only people who might stumble onto us are hunters or some peasant who needs to fish the Sava, which isn't frozen. I can get us around a Partisan camp late tonight, but I can't do anything about random hunters or fishermen. I hope it doesn't happen, but if they enter our camp, we will have to kill them silently."

Noack responded, "I see. The mission is critical for the safety of our men retreating so you are unfortunately correct. We will have to kill intruders or risk having the mission compromised. Get your feet checked, eat, and sleep as much as you like, Fritz; good job."

Fritz nodded positively and Noack reached down and patted the young man's shoulder as he and Ernst walked in a low crouch to a bush covered ravine. It was a small area in the woods but adequate for two or three men to stand without giving away their location to the enemy or other intruders.

Noack and Ernst stood erect in the little ravine and Noack spoke first, "Well, what do you think, Ernst?"

Ernst replied, "Speak freely, sir?"

Noack smiled and in a friendly manner said, "Of course, Ernst. I might get wounded or killed at any time and you will be in command. We can't have secrets."

Ernst smiled and said, "Well, sir, tonight will be the test, getting around the Partisan camp without a fight."

Noack, after a drink from his canteen, said, "Fritz will head back out an hour later than normal, you thirty minutes after Fritz, and the rest will follow in twenty minutes. Then Fritz can backtrack to you quickly and rest while you backtrack to us with the information for a decision. If Rudy is not back to you within thirty minutes, we are not coming and both of you are to double time it back to us. Understood?"

"Ja'wohl, sir."

"Good," responded Noack. "Ernst, I have another thought and I want your honest opinion. If Fritz is correct and even if it takes longer to blow the Šabac bridge, we will drop a lot of weight after the bridge is blown. We will move as fast as possible back along the same route on which we came. Of course, we will go very wide around any Partisan camp but at a much faster pace, which means we will need less rations to get to Visegrád, so I think we can go back to full rations and get back to Visegrád in three to four nights. What do you think?"

Thoughtfully, he replied, "Sir, I think it would be helpful for our stamina and strength, and we need it."

Noack said, "Glad you agree. We will start full rations today. Now, Ernst, go back and move the men one at a time into this ravine with ponchos except Fritz. Let him sleep. You can clean, inspect and dry fire his machine pistol for him and have each man service their own weapon. You then inspect them. Make sure the men have all the ammo they can carry for the three MP40 machine pistols, rifles, and all sidearms. I'll service mine back at my poncho."

"Yes, sir." Ernst left to start the weapon servicing. Noack followed behind him, both in a low crouch.

The weather was overcast but enough light to be seen by hunters or anyone unlucky enough to stumble into their camp. All men, except Fritz who knew more than us anyway, were told that except when in the ravine they had to talk in a whisper and walk in a crouch. All understood. Noack would brief everyone after Fritz and Ernst were on their way.

In the meantime, he would make his rounds, speaking to the guard on duty and stopping to answer questions from others. Then he told Ernst he was going to sleep. After full rations, about 1750 hours while there was a little light left, he told Ernst, "Wake Fritz so he can wash up, get his feet treated, and eat his rations. He will break camp at 1930 hours, with you behind him shortly thereafter. I will bring the group at 2010."

Noack went to his sleeping bag on a dry poncho, which was nice, but it was a little colder for daytime. He thought it was just above freezing.

After their first full ration meal in a while, they were all burping and smiling. As Fritz left to find a safe route, Ernst got each man to take his poncho to the ravine one at a time. The guard would sit close to the entrance to where the Commander would speak to them. After Ernst got the last man there, he left to get ready to follow Fritz's footsteps in the mud that were about to freeze. Noack passed him and wished him good luck.

Noack had about twenty minutes to brief the group about the

danger of going around a Communist Partisan camp. They needed to use hand signals man to man, absolute silence. These Partisans may even have Soviet advisors with them, which would make them more disciplined and they would have more alert guards posted. If not, there will be huge campfires, free flowing alcohol, female companions, and a party atmosphere. If we see and hear a party, we will be able to slip past their camp silently. He told the men sternly, "If we accidently overrun one of their guards, we cannot fire weapons. One of you cover his or her mouth while your buddy cuts their throat or strangles him or her. These women are big, stout, and as mean as Satan. These women have killed many of our Kameraden at Belgrade in support of the Soviet attack. Forget your feelings about women; these are killers. Don't hesitate! Kill her fast and quietly. Understood?"

"Ja'wohl, sir," they whispered quietly.

Noack responded, "You are rear guard. We will march in single file trying to step in the man's footsteps in front of you. Maintain absolute silence."

Rudy moved to the rear of the small column. They headed out in the partially frozen muddy trail left by Fritz and Ernst. It was still overcast with bits of moonlight every few minutes. This worried Oberleutnant Noack as they were good targets every few minutes, but he decided to push on. The temperature was dropping and a drizzle/snow combination started as they moved toward Šabac . About thirty minutes later as visibility increased, the drizzle turned into only snow. The temperature was now below thirty degrees. Noack saw a small stand of trees with tall bushes in the area. He held up his hand to stop the column, then whispered to Hans behind him to sign by hand to Rudy to follow them to the stand of trees. He then left the trail, going left into the trees. He went behind two large bushes that hid them from the trail.

Noack whispered to Hans, "Stand guard with my sidearm while I change into white camo, and then I will guard while you change. When Rudy gets here, you take the machine pistol and guard while he changes. Then we will resume the march. Ernst and Fritz will know to change. We will march in Ernst's trail until he comes back to brief us. Until then, once we are back on the trail, quiet will be our key word."

Within five minutes Rudy had slowly monitored their rear area as he backed into the trees. Hans took his machine pistol and stood guard as Rudy began to change. Rudy completed his change and relieved Hans. Noack whispered to Rudy, "Make sure you are especially observant to our rear area as we move closer to the Partisan camp. If they discover Fritz, they will try to encircle us. If we hear Fritz fire two bursts, Ernst and Fritz know we will each go toward the Sava on our own. Try to find a rowboat and row or run toward the Drina and safety. We will each try to meet up at the first possible safe area available near the Drina. Understand?"

"Ja'wohl, Herr Oberleutnant."

Noack repeated, "Don't try to reach Hans and me, run toward the Sava and hide in brush." Rudy nodded his head in the affirmative. Noack said, "Hans will follow my footprints."

Following this, all had white hoods, making the snow less irritable. Rudy obtained some of the extra ammo from Noack's pack and the three of them reentered the trail, which was becoming harder to see. Rudy scanned the rear area as best he could through the falling snow. He laughed at himself, thinking at least the snow will cover all the yellow stains by that big bush. He moved forward behind Hans and Noack. They marched for about forty-minutes, hearing no gunfire or noise. Abruptly Noack stopped so suddenly that Hans bumped him but kept quiet. They both saw Ernst walking toward them. As he arrived, Rudy had also moved up quickly from the rear and all four were together. Ernst whispered they didn't have time to rest as they were very close to a loud Partisan camp with huge bonfires and lots of loud noise but with many perimeter guards. Fritz was changing our route around them now. We were going due east for about a half mile, then turning right toward Šabac . This would get us around the Partisans and to a hidden campsite before dawn. Ernst said, "Follow me, sir." Noack nodded his head affirmatively and they set out with Ernst in the lead. They reached the spot where Fritz had backtracked from and dropped Partisan trash. The men cut left to the route due east. Knowing the snow would have their trail completely covered in minutes, Noack didn't take any precautions. Ernst slowed his pace once they were about a hundred yards past the intersection as he knew the tired, cold middle-aged Commander was having difficulty keeping the pace. Ernst would do nothing to embarrass a man he admired, a man who was serving in his second damned war. As the three caught up to Ernst, Ernst addressed the Commander. "Sir, I twisted my ankle and I just have to go a bit slower." Noack suggested a break for Hans to look at his ankle. "No, sir," replied Ernst, "We don't have much time till daylight." Noack nodded affirmatively and Ernst led on with a slow limping appearance. They reached another bit of Partisan trash lightly covered with snow. After a second or two, Ernst turned right and began to head parallel with the Sava toward Šabac . A few minutes later, Noack, knowing that Ernst and Rudy were carrying the heavy explosives and supplies, machine pistols, and ammo, he asked Hans if he could carry the Panzerfaust for a while. Hans replied, "Happy to, sir, all the way." Noack smiled and said, "Thanks, Hans." They moved on. Ernst was about ten feet ahead and waved back, come to him. Ernst happily whispered, "I saw Fritz over there," pointing to trees and high brush to the left. They joined Fritz without worrying about their trail as it would disappear within minutes in the intensifying snow.

They immediately followed their routine without the need for the slit trench till morning, if then. Fritz, Ernst, and the Oberleutnant met and talked in whispers while Hans started on Ernst's ankle. He said nothing as he saw his ankle appeared normal. Looking at him sternly, Ernst said, "Tape it up tightly and new dry socks." Without a change in facial expression, Hans said, "Ja'wohl, Stabsfeldwebel. We all get new dry socks tonight." Noack had been busy listening to Fritz whispering his report and had paid no attention to the exchange between Ernst and Hans.

According to Fritz, they would have to zig and zag between little clusters of farm houses, outbuildings, small farm roads, and creeks or streams the rest of the way, but that shouldn't be a problem at night until an hour before dawn. He also reported they may have to borrow rowboats where available. Noack put the word out man to man in a whisper that if they left about 2000 hours with Fritz going out at 1930 and Ernst at 1940 it would take about two or three more nights to get within a distance that Ernst, Rudy, and Fritz could reconnoiter the area at the bridge. We would then plan the destruction of the traffic bridge crossing the Sava and would execute the order to blow the bridge on one night depending on Ernst and Rudy's plan of action. Noack told the men, "Now Ernst will give you the guard roster and the rest can sleep" and in low tones said, "I'm looking forward to full rations again at 1730 hours." The men all nodded their heads in agreement. After Ernst finished assigning guard shifts with Rudy on first, the others carefully unfolded their ponchos so one portion covered the ground, then their sleeping bag with the other half of the poncho over the sleeping bag. They took off their white covered helmets and put them above their heads on the ground. Their heads were covered with the white hood pulled tight at the top of their foreheads and chins. They were invisible to even their passing guard.

At 1700 hours Hans was gently waking his tired Commander.

After washing his face with a clean rag from Hans, who had dampened it, he cleaned his hands. Hans then checked both of his feet. Hans told him the corn had come off in the plaster. He then cleaned the area with an antiseptic and put iodine on the area and a small band-aid over his left little toe. He then gave the Oberleutnant three socks, two for the left foot and one for the right. Noack thanked him as he was leaving to examine and treat, if needed, the others. At 1730 they ate their full but cold rations with powdered milk or water. After this, Ernst and Rudy went around helping with a weapons check and making sure each man had all the ammo and hand grenades he could carry. Ernst and Rudy also told each man that silence and face to face hand signals were critical on the trail if they were to be successful in their mission.

Fritz set out at 1950 late under overcast skies with visibility limited to about ten to fifteen feet. It was snowing lightly with the temperature dropping. Ernst was a few minutes late due to Hans needing to finish his blister treatment. Ernst moved out at 2005 hours. Noack, Hans, and Rudy left at 2015.

With visibility so limited, absolute silence enroute was essential. Ernst was startled when Fritz came into sight about twenty minutes out. In a whisper Fritz told him about half a mile ahead there was a water source for a large farming area about twenty feet off to the right. He left local trash he got out of a container near a closed little store. Fritz said, "Better fill all canteens and containers. I also found a Belgrade newspaper from last week, which I think is in Russian."

Ernst replied, "I speak Russian. That's great, Fritz, maybe Oberleutnant Noack and I can find some news and information about what the hell is going on in terms of the Bolsheviki trying to pursue our retreating Kameraden."

Fritz answered, "I hope so, but it looks like Greek to me."

Fritz turned and stepped back into the light snow, very poor visibility, and darkness and moved out on the animal trail. Ernst turned and walked slowly back toward the column having four or five feet of ground visible. He followed his own footsteps. After about ten minutes he thought to himself the hell with this. He spotted a tree stump a few feet to the right of what used to be an animal trail and sat and waited. About ten minutes later Noack appeared to his right about a foot in front of him. Noack sensed a presence and was reaching for his sidearm when Ernst grabbed his hand, "Sir, it's Ernst." Noack calmly whispered, "Good, wasn't sure." Ernst motioned for them to gather around close. He then told them about the water ahead. Later he and the Commander, after they found Fritz at the campsite, would discuss the news from Belgrade. Ernst asked Noack for permission to stay closer as pointman due to such limited visibility. Noack agreed and they moved forward toward the available potable water source.

In about thirty minutes Ernst found the trash Fritz had left marking in the snow where to turn right. Noack told Ernst to go with Hans to fill the canteens while the rest waited at the trail. In about fifteen minutes Ernst and Hans returned with the filled canteens and one container. Noack signaled to restart the march to the campsite. In less than an hour Ernst held up his right hand to stop. He found more local trash pointing left. They left the trail and within two minutes found Fritz waving at them. He had found a very secluded place far enough away from the trail and any paths. It would be safe during the day and in unlimited visibility as they went down into a nice deep ravine with high brush around the crest. When all five were accounted for, Ernst and Rudy built a three poncho shelter that would blackout a flashlight while Ernst read the Russian news that might affect them, translating into German as he read silently to himself. Rudy left for his guard duty. Ernst would later brief him, who would whisper it to the other two. No one had any foot complaints or medical problems other than fatigue and muscle soreness so Hans was going to relax until about 1700 when he would perform the men's foot check. All prepared their poncho/sleeping bag bed while Rudy posted the guard roster verbally in a whisper to all. Ernst told all of them that they would inspect, wipe down and oil as needed all sidearms, one rifle, and machine pistols after rations before sundown and be moving out at about 2000 hours. He then returned to their shelter with Oberleutnant Noack to discuss plans. The week old Belgrade newspaper that Fritz had found in the trash was a blessing. It stated

that the Russian (Soviet) and Combined Tito HQ in Belgrade had

ordered the only Tito Brigade in the Šabac area to return to

Belgrade two days ago. It was also mentioned that the Partisans,

including a new brigade of Muslim Partisans, were operating in

Yugoslavia. They were searching out German troops for total

destruction. It went on to brag about what the Soviets and Tito were

doing to help Yugoslavia and they had plans to fully integrate the

Communist Partisans into all government positions before the

Soviets withdrew from Yugoslavia. Of course, the newspaper said

the Soviets were working closely with the great friend of the Soviet

Union, Marshal Tito. Noack laughed softly and said, "They are not

too bright. Before the Soviets are ten miles up the road, Tito and his

Communist Partisans will claim all the glory was theirs. Wait and see.

But the hell with that, the important thing is those drunken

Communist bastards will be the only ones there when we arrive. If

we reconnoiter and then strike on a bad weather night, they will be

in their camps or temporary quarters drunk on their asses. You know, Ernst, in my military history readings, I learned that during the American Revolution, when down on his luck like we are now, George Washington defeated the pride of the Prussian Army, which changed the war."

Ernst asked, "How did he do that, sir?"

Noack related how, "on a bad weather night of freezing and heavy snow, he crossed a river and marched during the night to the town where the Prussian soldiers were. It had been published in a paper where the new Prussian troops, who were supporting England, were garrisoned. General Washington hired some prostitutes to be in town when the Prussians arrived. The Madam sent dispatches to the General, telling him that the Prussian troops were taking a liking to them and the beer, wine, and whiskey. Washington knew that this was his chance for a big victory over well trained regulars by his ill fed militia. Washington and his militia struck early on a freezing morning with snow and ice everywhere. His poorly armed men caught the Prussian officers in bed with George's girls and NCOs and troops passed out from drink. When more and more casualties became apparent, the Senior Officer surrendered the Prussian troops. This rallied the Americans to fight on to total victory. Well, Ernst, I only care about one bridge and getting all of us back to Visegrád and safety. We have already crossed our river, the Drina, putting us on the west side of the Sava. We will check things out and wait in hiding for rain or snow, then strike about 0330 hours one night. Pursuing troops will have to come across with vehicles and equipment from Belgrade, slowing them significantly." He held up his hand in a fake toast saying, "here's to General Washington."

"Here, here," responded Ernst.

"Ernst, go brief Rudy and get some sleep. See you about 1730."

Ernst dismantled the poncho shelter so Noack could make his bed. He departed and went on to brief Rudy quietly and then made sure the guard was in place near the entrance to the ravine. Rudy had set up a trip wire tied to cans about twenty feet down the other end, which would be time for him to fire his machine pistol into the void as it was in snow and darkness.

Except for one guard that changed every two hours, all slept in a sleeping bag under their poncho top and then a layer of snow. They started getting up slowly around 1700 hours, including Noack. At that time their routine started, foot check, inspect weapons and gear, eat full rations, and prepare for a short briefing before departure.

Again, Fritz set out at about 2000 hours, followed by Ernst, and less than thirty minutes after Ernst, Noack, Hans, and Rudy followed. Noack estimated that it was about thirty degrees Fahrenheit, snowing, not cold enough to freeze ground snow quickly to ice but cold enough to save footsteps even if visibility were two to three feet. He would use his poncho and squat down to block out his flashlight illuminating hard to see footprints, but this would slow them down. Again, he thought, "Slow but safe is better than fast and dead. Back on half rations tomorrow."

They trudged on for four hours slowly with breaks every hour or so. A few minutes after 0140 hours Ernst met them, holding up his right hand to stop. He whispered something to Oberleutnant Noack and turned, leaving quickly. By this time Rudy had caught up with Hans and Noack. There was a good size log off the trail, toward which Noack waved for them to sit. He sat and began in a low voice, "Fritz has our campsite. We go about a mile forward and turn left at local trash to the left on an animal trail for about a half mile, then right at the trash for about a quarter mile on the right. We should arrive about 0500 hours, which is well before dawn. Questions?"

Rudy answered, "No, sir."

Noack stated in a calm voice, "All is in order. Let's go."

Noack arose and Hans followed. Being the rear guard duty, Rudy stayed seated for a few minutes after the Commander left. He rose after about five minutes. A fresh chew of tobacco was in his mouth and, just in case, he piled snow over where he had spat. With excellent night vision, he had no trouble following the two and scanning the rear area and the rear right and left areas as he moved. As the snow began to lighten up, his visibility improved, and this allowed him to catch up too fast, and shortly before Noack and Hans met Ernst at the trash marker, he was about ten feet behind carrying the Panzerfaust. Rudy thought, "The chance of seeing a Soviet T34 in this area is less than seeing an Irish leprechaun," laughing quietly to himself.

Noack signaled to both of them to come with him as Ernst became visible, waving to them. Ernst said all was clear and they were about forty-five minutes from the campsite off the trail. It was pretty level and he would drop local trash if there were any holes or other impediments. He set out and the three followed in the usual formation. With no warnings seen from Ernst, they made excellent time. They arrived to a smile and greeting from Fritz, a great recon man. Noack was pleased and let Fritz direct him to a nice sunken area surrounded by bushy white small trees. There was room for four, which was perfect as one would always be on a rotating guard shift. Hans and Rudy could alternate using a sleeping bag so Fritz could sleep in after getting back from a predawn area recon once he briefed Noack. While Hans checked Rudy and his own feet, Fritz reported to their Commander with the Senior NCO listening carefully.

Fritz spoke freely as ordered, stating, "I had to borrow a rowboat to get across a little stream ahead. I put it back just as I found it and the snow will erase my use. This whole area is full of farm dirt roads, streams, and ponds. Creeks flow into streams and most go into the Sava. When we finish, Sir, with your approval, I'm going out to find a footbridge to cross the stream. Should be back before full light. I'll stay close to cover. With everything white, no one will see me anyway even if they were looking for me, and in white camo we are in pretty good shape."

Noack thanked him and said, "Grab some powdered milk and crackers and get going."

"Yes, sir."

He moved down to Hans to get something on a blister while making his milk and eating his crackers.

Rudy had taken first guard. Within ten minutes Fritz was gone. Ernst commented to Noack, "Fritz is like a ghost. He appears and then he disappears."

Noack responded, "Well, I'm glad as hell you found him when you were seeking volunteers with the Major."

"Yes, sir. Me, too!"

Noack asked, "How did you find Willie?"

"Sir, when he heard we were looking for volunteers to accept a top secret dangerous mission, he stood up and shouted, 'Me, sir.' I took him outside and Private Thomsen told me he had been in an infantry company in a battalion that was part of von Weichs' Army Group in Belgrade. He said the fighting against Tito's troops, the Soviet troops, Bulgarian troops, and dirty Partisans was horrific. He said about twelve thousand Wehrmacht troops knew the only way out was to Šabac and the bridge. The boy is surprised he is alive. All his buddies were killed between Belgrade and the bridge. He wound up in the center of the rear guard when they got to the bridge in Šabac and crossed." He also said that he overheard some field grade officer telling a company commander that approximately twelve thousand fled starting on October 19 as no communication was possible to von Weichs' Army Group. Division and Brigade Commanders assumed they had been overrun, killed, or captured. There was building to building and floor to floor combat in Belgrade. Word evidently went out for all units to break clear and retreat fighting a rear guard section to Šabac , regroup on the western side and proceed to Sarajevo for orders.

Ernst continued, "I know reports from a Private won't have much weight with OKH, but he swears that he saw thousands of our troops lying dead along the road to the Šabac bridge, but when you compare Private Thomsen's estimate of losses with the Field Grade Officer's instructions to a company commander, it makes sense. The Oberst had opined that he estimated about nine thousand Wehrmacht troops made it across the bridge with four or five hundred lying dead on the east side of the bridge and on the bridge. Maybe a few hundred on the west side as they marched toward Sarajevo from mortar fire down below the bridge."

Noack said, "Damn, now it does make some sense. I'll explain tomorrow. I'm too tired to talk. Also, Ernst, if I don't make it, tell whoever you report to that I requested Willie, Hans, and Max be promoted one rank, Fritz to Unteroffizier, Karl to Obergefreiter, and I wholeheartedly endorse you and Rudy to Leutnant and, last but not least, Otto to Stabsfeldwebel. You have all exceeded my expectations to say the least."

Ernst responded, "Sir, thank you from my heart but, sir, Rudy and I don't wish to be officers."

Noack smiled broadly and stated, "Do you really think I did? Welcome to the world of rolling with the punches, Ernst. You'd better pray I make it back, and I'll hold your promotions down to Hauptfeldwebel for you both. That's a great position. I really enjoyed it."

Ernst, still shook, said, "Thank you, sir. That sounds great and it will help our families."

Noack smiled and said, "I'm going to sleep till 1700 hours."

Ernst left to check on everything and, when satisfied, he laid down, too. Guards changed shifts without incident and all got some needed rest. About 0800 hours the guard heard Fritz and his bird call and walked toward it. Fritz came into camp and went straight to his sleeping bag after visiting a distant bush that had a faint yellow stain in the snow. It suddenly got brighter as he relieved himself.

When Noack awoke about 1710, he washed off and saw that Fritz was already up and talking with Otto about something. When he saw the Commander, Fritz broke off his conversation with Otto and walked to the Commander. Noack said, "Let's sit here and wait on Ernst. He will be right back." Fritz and Noack were barely seated when Ernst joined them. Noack said, "Fritz, what did you find?"

"Sir, when we leave tonight, we can save three miles down to a foot bridge if we take the rowboat, but we won't be able to get the rowboat back to the other side."

Noack said, "That's okay. Leave some local trash in the boat. When the farmer finds his boat, he won't look for us." Ernst and Fritz laughed quietly and Noack smiled.

"What else," Noack asked.

"Sir, there are boats everywhere. If we went straight to the Sava and took a motorboat, we could be at the bridge in a couple of hours."

Noack smiled and held up his hand to stop, saying, "Thanks, Corporal Peiper, but too many things could go wrong. We shall stick with slow but safe. Understood?"

Both responded with a "Ja'wohl, Oberleutnant."

Ernst thought to himself, knowing that he had thought it was a good idea, thank God for this old Hare. Experience and sound judgment beats ambition and fleeting glory. Hell, we might survive this mission.

Since it would only be a short distance to the stream, Noack wanted to make sure the farmhouse was dark and all were in bed. They moved out together with Fritz at the point, then Ernst a few feet behind, followed by Noack and Hans with Rudy close behind. They were like a column of ducks going down to water. They left at 2100 hours in light snow with a chilly but tolerable temperature of thirty-one degrees Fahrenheit by Noack's thermometer.

At the rowboat they quietly put it back in the water and got in. First, Fritz dumped local trash, which included discarded local mail, in the boat and handed an oar to Hans, keeping the other one. Both rowed to the opposite shore. As they beached the rowboat, Ernst checked to make sure there were no Wehrmacht items in the boat, only a neighbor's trash. They moved out, having saved about two plus hours of marching. With light snow and a reasonable temperature, they could make good time through this agricultural area barring Partisans. At this point Fritz left immediately with Ernst following in ten minutes and Noack and Hans behind by ten minutes and Rudy, as rear guard, five minutes back. They zigged and zagged around farmhouses, outbuildings, equipment, and ponds for six hours.

Counting short breaks, about 0400 hours Ernst came back and said Fritz had their campsite picked out about fifty yards to the right of the trail in a dense tree and brush stand. About thirty more minutes, Fritz had done it again, a really dense area with high brush. After setting up with time to spare, they were all invisible in their white camo. All but the guard were in their snow covered beds before light gradually dimly illuminated the trees. It was going to be a dark, gloomy day, which was good news. Most farm families would stay indoors on a February day like this except for brief necessary duties. As long as they were quiet, they were safe.

Before rations, Noack Fritz, and Ernst met. Noack said to both, "Fritz, I want you, when we get within ten miles of Šabac (signposts for farmers were seen by him frequently), to find three good fallback positions we can use to retreat after the bridge is blown. The closest to Šabac should be about a quarter mile from the bridge. It should be a deep ditch or ravine with good cover but an excellent field of fire toward the bridge from where our enemies will come seeking engagement. The next fallback position should be a half mile behind the first going on our route back to Visegrád. The third fallback position should be about two miles to the rear of the second. Questions?"

"No, sir,"

"Ernst, you will brief the men tomorrow individually." He went on, stating, "When Ernst is satisfied with the selection of positions as to depth, cover and field of fire, you will hide the spare ammo and rations in these three fallback positions after we have established our last campsite about four to six miles from Šabac. Then on a night with heavy snow or just very poor visibility, we will move forward, stocking all three positions while you, Ernst, and Rudy reconnoiter the bridge. If you and Rudy are satisfied that you can blow it, the four of us will go in about 0200 hours on the next night with heavy snow or poor visibility and blow that damned bridge. Hans will stay at the first fallback position to cover us as we return and in case we need medical treatment. As Hans and any wounded retreat to the second position, the remaining men will fight a rear guard action from there to the next fallback position. Hans at the second position will have rigged a poncho with two poles so any wounded not able to walk can be carried or dragged to the last fallback position where we will make our last stand."

After a moment, Noack continued, "Naturally as we leave the first and second positions, we will bring the ammo left with us. In the poor visibility that night we should be far enough ahead to be safe. We know where we are going and have a great field of fire, and they won't have either. Make sure everyone keeps an eye out for poles or limbs or boat oars that we can leave at position two. Questions?"

Ernst spoke first, "Sir, after the bridge goes, Ernst and I can carry all the spare ammo and we should be able to move rapidly. Sir, what if one or more of us can't be carried if seriously wounded?"

Noack stated firmly, "We will stand and fight at the last position or at our last campsite, whichever is more advantageous to us. If I'm killed, Ernst, it will be your decision to make. If we get back as far as the last campsite, I think we will make it. They will have no idea about our direction of retreat in heavy snow or rain with poor visibility. We will know exactly how to find shelter and safety, fallback position one, and so on. Once we have reconned the bridge, we will wait it out for the right weather. That's the night we will strike. Remember, George?"

Fritz looked puzzled. Noack patted his shoulder and said, "Ernst can tell you later about a great soldier named George. Let's go eat some crackers and have some milk."

After all their ingrained routines had been completed, Fritz moved out at 2000 hours with Ernst close behind by ten minutes, followed by Noack, Hans, and Rudy fifteen minutes later. Again, they zigged and zagged around homes, rural stores, ponds, equipment storage, and penned up animals. At 0400 hours they spotted Ernst ahead holding up his hand. He whispered Fritz had found an ideal last campsite at a shutdown construction site with deep trenches overgrown with high brush plus a large hill from which the Commander could use his binoculars to look at the Sava and the outskirts of Šabac . As Rudy caught up, he had stayed out three minutes behind the Commander, Ernst said, "It's about fifteen minutes away and a little over four miles to Šabac according to the last road sign he spotted."

Noack said, "Excellent. Let's get there," and they all moved out together single file behind Ernst.

About 0450 hours they were in their last camp. Before their recon of the Šabac Bridge it would be a day or so depending on the weather. There were large concrete culverts were sitting above ground with high brush surrounding them. A lot of hiding places for a rear guard if retreating or if they had no choice but to stand and fight. Noack was again pleased and thankful for Corporal Peiper and Master/Sergeant Steiner, and two good soldiers who knew their jobs. He turned to Hans and said, "I'll need two aspirin and a packet of those cough drops in your pack each day. Also make sure each man has a packet of cough drops in his pocket by tonight. We cannot have me or anyone else coughing day or night. We need to be as silent as humanly possible from this moment on."

Hans, nodding yes, handed him two aspirin and a packet of strong cough drops. He then left to see if anyone needed anything. He had selected a big culvert lying above a long, deep trench that appeared to have been dug many months before. He set up his medical supplies in the culvert and then went to each man, advising them to come to the culvert now or about 1700 hours. He would stay in the culvert.

Evidently the war had halted construction of something that would have been a commercial center for Šabac and area farm folk.

Now it was their haven for a day or two.

Noack took one of the aspirin and saved the other one for 1700 hours. He also relaxed as a very potent cough drop eased his urge to cough. He, Ernst, and Fritz stopped as they entered another very large culvert behind the medic's culvert. Noack thanked them for an excellent campsite, totally abandoned for many months by the look of things, but they still needed to maintain all their routines, slit trench, bury all trash and cover with old brush. He relayed this to Ernst, who nodded.

Noack then said, "Gentlemen, you have done a magnificent job, but now it's life or death starting tonight. Keep doing your best and we all may make it home." Everyone nodded. He continued, "Ernst, tonight I won't go; instead take Rudy so you both are fully aware of all aspects of our pending attack. The assignment for tonight is to select the third fallback position, hide ammo, and hopefully find two poles for Hans' stretcher. If you still have time and it looks safe, move forward and try to find the second fallback position. Get back here before sunup. Understood?"

"Yes, sir," as the Senior NCO spoke for both.

"Good. Fritz, go set up your bed and ask Rudy to post the guard."

Fritz responded, "Ja'wohl, Herr Oberleutnant."

Noack left, looking forward to a good sleep. For once it wasn't raining or snowing, but it was overcast with the temperature just above freezing and rising slowly.

Noack returned to Ernst face to face and said, "I need to share more information with you in case you take command in the next few days. When the young Major briefed me back at our camp near Sarajevo, he gave me the last intelligence they had received from Abwehr in Berlin. According to the Major, and it matches what I and maybe you saw on our way through Yugoslavia freeing up trapped Kameraden; Berlin says that Soviet troops are trying to pursue and capture Wehrmacht soldiers trying to reach Austria through Hungary. Ivan will stay on the right side of the Sava moving toward Hungary. The Bulgarians, Tito's troops, and the Communist Partisans and now even Muslim Partisans led by Chetniks will be pushing along the western and central areas of Yugoslavia searching for any lost Wehrmacht troops. Do you recall the first skirmish we got into near the Bulgarian border headed to Skopje, the lake near Dojransko?

Ernst interrupted, "Sir, I will never forget it. My best friend, Bruno, from my hometown, Bad Vilbel, was killed right next to me. Then we were ordered to break it off and get back on course toward Skopje where our troops were trapped."

Noack responded, "Exactly! This was maybe a week before Belgrade fell."

Ernst nodded and whispered, "Jah."

Noack asked, "What did we see after our fight at Skopje as we moved toward Prishtina with the Kameraden we freed?"

"Sir, we kept seeing trash and took sniper fire and then our enemy turned west toward Albania as we moved toward Prishtina."

Noack responded, "Yes, and if Abwehr is right, after Belgrade fell, the Soviets went after those fleeing to Hungary from the Belgrade area via a different route. Those Kameraden who headed for Šabac , those lucky enough to cross the Sava were left to the combined forces of Bulgaria, Tito, and those damned Partisans."

Noack continued, "You know the Sava flows down from the Julian Alps and is our road map to Austria once we join the division at Sarajevo."

"Yes, sir."

"Well, that means the Soviets will be on our right across the Sava going north and Tito and his allies will be on our left, so we have to stay in the center. Once we blow the bridge, we must stay close to the route we came on. If we make it back, let's just hope Division Operations has enough sense to stay to the center with frequent serpentine moves."

Ernst responded, "Absolutely, sir."

Noack continued, "Right now, Ernst, let's just get the bridge and get back to Visegrád. I'll see you at 1730 for rations. Go ahead and see if Rudy has things under control. I'm going to bed down here in this culvert."

"Ja'wohl, Herr Oberleutnant," Ernst affirmed as he left to

check the small area being used as their encampment.

Later, as they finished their rations, Noack spoke softly to Fritz and Ernst, "You know, Bulgaria and the Chetniks were our allies. Now they're fighting with Ivan. What kind of loyalty did their leaders have? Not much! To hell with them, but remember we don't want to kill civilians, especially farmers or children, do we?"

Both responded, "No, sir."

"Good. With God's help we will be home ourselves trying to forget all these things and, believe me, we don't want to remember children or old folks who died on this damn bridge. Correct?"

"Ja'wohl, Herr Oberleutnant."

Noack told them, "Go check your weapons, get the spare ammo for storing at position three. Don't forget to try to find some poles." Fritz and Ernst silently saluted and left.

Noack walked around and quietly looked things over and told Hans that he would stand watch for him and they would change every three hours starting at 0200 hours. Noack said he would take the first shift and had kept his machine pistol as Rudy and Ernst both had MP-40s. Fritz could carry the extra ammo for position three.

After Ernst, Rudy, and Fritz left headed parallel with the meandering Sava, which was a problem, toward Šabac . One minute they would be closer to the Sava and then five minutes later they would be a safer distance from it. It wasn't raining or snowing, but snow was on the ground and visibility was limited so it was fairly safe. Civilians were in bed and there were no military regulars ahead of them, only Partisans who were probably drinking heavily by now and looking at the available women. If the good Oberleutnant was right, they could count on that.

Fritz was out a little ahead of Ernst and Rudy as he was the recon specialist. Ernst and Rudy walked right into him as he was in a crouch. He held up his hand silently to stop, pointing off to the left. The three backed up about fifty yards off the trail. Fritz told them softly that two men were putting up their gear and a rowboat alongside of a barn. We had evidently zigged too far and were a short walk from the Sava and approximately less than three miles from our target. He said about half a mile or less up the farm road off to the right was a dense area that they should inspect for the possibility of position three.

After waiting about ten minutes off their feet on a large downed tree, they walked back toward the barn. Fritz told them to hold up with a hand signal. He then cautiously approached the barn barely visible to Ernst and Rudy. When he came back, he had a big smile, two oars, and a bag of new local trash to mark jump off points. Rudy and Ernst smiled and took one of the oars and the sack of local trash. Rudy whispered to Fritz, "Excellent work, Fritz." They pushed on, three white ghosts, two carrying an oar and MP40s with Fritz carrying the bag of trash and ammo in his pack.

Within thirty minutes they were off the trail with no trash dropped as it wasn't needed. The site was well within a dense area, high brush and trees and a natural dell or lower area. When crouching or in their sleeping bags, they couldn't be seen from any area. Both the farm road and trails were seventy to eighty yards away on all sides. Ernst and Rudy hid the oars and extra ammo over which they placed dead fallen brush. Rudy handed Fritz a small limb with lots of even smaller limbs with plenty of firm leaves. When they got close to the road, they would walk in their incoming footsteps and Fritz would erase all footprints from the farm road. With this done, they headed back to the campsite with Fritz bringing up the rear brushing footprints for about fifty yards. They were safely back in camp at 0500 hours. Noack was on guard as Fritz blew the bird call one time and Noack walked toward them, happy that his boys were safely back.

Noack awoke Fritz about 0700 hours as he wanted a report from them without a longer delay. Fritz washed off his face quickly and joined Noack and the others. They went into his headquarters, his culvert.

Ernst,t as Senior NCO, started first, "Sir, things went well. First Fritz borrowed a couple of oars. The materials Hans will need to rig a stretcher are in place. Spare ammo and med supplies are at fallback position three."

Noack, breaking in, said "How many people did you see?"

Ernst advised, "Only two putting up their rowboat. We were near the Sava."

Noack, apparently pleased, said, "That's a good sign. What else, Rudy?"

"Sir, position three is very well hidden. It's in a small dell so if crouched or lying down even in good visibility we can't be seen. We could fight off a lot of Partisans with these MP40's, a rifle, and grenades."

"Let's hope that won't happen. Our only mission is to blow the bridge and get our asses back to safety," replied Noack.

"Ja'wohl, sir," offered Ernst.

"More?"

Ernst looked at Fritz and Rudy as their senior in rank and said, "Sir, Fritz has a bag of trash and a new newspaper, but it's not in Russian, Czech, or German. It's a Serbian paper. Makes sense if only Yugoslavian Partisans replaced Tito's troops recently in Šabac."

Noack interrupted, saying, "I can't speak it, but October,

November, and twenty-four days of December in this place I can read enough to get the gist of their written messages."

While Noack had been talking, Fritz was digging through the trash bag and handed him the newspaper. The Commander said, "Good job, men. Have some milk or water and crackers and get some sleep. Rudy, Hans will wake you in about three hours to take guard, then Fritz, and Ernst last."

"Ja'wohl, Herr Oberleutnant."

The men left for a snack and bed. Noack sat up in the culvert thinking about home in Cottbus and wondered if Soviet troops were there yet. The sun wasn't shining, but it broke through enough to light up the gloomy overcast adequately for him to see this three page newspaper.

God, he hated this place, not the people but the atheist communists that would and are already in charge of their government. He felt that all average people everywhere were basically good, hardworking, and just wanted to care for their families and be left alone. It was the damned politicians, even the ones claiming to be religious; as many become corrupted over time, but the atheist communists are the worst. He thought, "God help us from these politicians in all countries that send boys and men out to kill each other while they live like royalty and even communicate with each other. We are just their pawns." Then he thought, "That's enough of that, Kurt." He opened the wrinkled paper up and was surprised fish hadn't been wrapped in it. That's a break! Any little thing that was positive would brighten his day.

He started trying to decipher the news, first the weather. As best as he could make out, the next seventy-two hours would be a cold snap with temperatures not above thirty-two degrees Fahrenheit in the day and night with snow for two days and nights, light snow starting in twenty-four hours, then moderate snow and in the forty-eight hours moderate to heavy snow all night long with wind and poor visibility. The last night of this system, the traffic conditions would be hazardous after three p.m. through the night before clearing the next day. He thought, "Damn, this is good -- not as good as Washington had, but it's our chance to get in and get the hell out."

By this time, it was Rudy's turn to relieve Hans. Noack walked over to Hans and told him to wake Rudy but give him a few minutes to relieve you. He told Hans, "Get some sleep and I'll see you about 1700 hours." Both crawled into their sleeping bags and slept soundly. At 1715 hours Hans gently touched the old man's shoulder and said, "Sir, it's time to get up."

He got out of his sleeping bag and scooted out of the culvert to wash his face and hands with a bowl of water Hans had brought for him with soap and clean rags. Noack spoke softly, "Thank you, Hans. You make me feel like a human again." Hans said, "You're welcome, sir. Better let me look at your feet before you get busy." Hans treated two blisters and the remnants of his left little toe corn and said, "Here are your fresh socks, sir. You only need two socks as the left little toe looks much better." He cleaned up the mess and headed to the slit trench he had dug on arrival to bury the waste.

Noack went over to where Ernst was and joined him. They ate their meager rations together as Noack briefed them on the news from the paper, the weather for the next seventy-two hours. He told them that tonight he wanted them to move the oars from position three to position two and the medical supplies needed to stop bleeding and morphine to position one. Also, he needed a detailed description of the terrain around position one. If they got this done tonight, they would move to position three tomorrow night. Since we are so close, he told them, other than guard duty and checking weapons, relax until 2300 hours when they would move out. He said, "Stick with single file with Fritz as point."

Noack returned to his culvert to rest before they left and he would take the first shift at guard at 2300 hours with Hans relieving him at 0200 hours.

Time seems to move faster as you get older. Noack thought Hans was kidding when he touched his shoulder and said, "Sorry, sir, it's 0500." Noack said, "I'm sorry, too, " as he got out of his culvert, wiped his eyes, and accepted the MP40. The Commander had been on guard duty for about forty-five minutes when he heard the bird call. He moved toward his incoming men. He asked Rudy to take guard so Ernst and Fritz could brief him.

Ernst and Fritz sat down inside Noack's culvert. After he sat on his bedding, Ernst started, "Sir, the oars are in position two with ammo and the medical supplies in position one as ordered. Fritz can better describe the terrain."

Fritz said, "Sir, our first fallback position is elevated from the farm road on our left running parallel to the Sava. The bridge can be easily seen and with binoculars it's up close. Stabsfeldwebel Steiner was able to select the positions under the western side of the bridge where they will place the charges. Also, position one is deep enough for us to stand and fire and toss grenades downhill. About ten or twelve feet downslope toward the road there is an animal trail, very small but adequate for single file, that runs across in front of us west to east and leads to the farm road at the Sava."

Noack broke in, "Thank you, Corporal. Go relieve Rudy and have him report to me now." Fritz saluted silently after getting out of the culvert and went to find Rudy, who was out of sight. While they were waiting on Rudy to arrive, Ernst said, "Sir, there is something I didn't want to discuss in front of Fritz until you approved, if you do."

Noack said, "Go on."

Ernst stated, "While selecting the probable sites for our explosives, I saw something very interesting on the other side of the river. There are lots of boats tied up on the shore on both sides. On the eastern side very near the bridge are petrol storage tanks. It would be easy to get up from the water, fire our one Panzerfaust which you wisely brought expecting a T34 or some other possible use. Well, we have a definite use, sir. As quick as Fritz is, while we finish placing the charges and running the wire back in the direction of position one, Fritz could row across, hide under the bridge until your signal, perhaps the bird call. When Rudy and I are set to detonate the charges, you signal Fritz. He will go up the little incline from the shore, fire the Panzerfaust into the storage tank and lob a grenade in to enlarge the rupture with its burning contents draining out. He can return back across in the boat, rowing over to where we were in hiding with the detonator. As soon as Fritz is clear of the bridge and on shore, in sight, I will detonate the charges on your order."

Noack interrupted Ernst, "No, we will wait until Fritz is with us to detonate the charges."

Ernst responded, "Yes, sir. Then we will head back to position one and prepare for a fight or movement to position two. Also, they will be so busy with fire trucks and volunteers trying to put out the massive fire, the guard on the western side will be totally occupied trying to keep traffic stopped before driving into the River Sava. The western end of the bridge will be hanging down into the river where the current is the strongest. This will put stress on the remaining structure. The longer they wait to bring heavy equipment from Belgrade over the river near Belgrade, the more damage will be done to the hanging remnants. The men on the eastern side will not have time to come across in boats for at least a few hours. People on the west side are mainly farmers. They will be watching the fire across the river, wondering how it knocked down their part of the bridge. As they watch, we will return to position one and, if possible, back to position two. "

Noack told Ernst, "Excellent work and plan. After we get to position three tonight, I want you and Fritz to take me up to position one and I'll look over the bridge and petrol tanks. Then you and I will refine the plan for the following night if the weather gets bad enough. Have Rudy set up the guard schedule and get some rest."

Ernst said, "Thank you, sir," saluted after standing and returned to where Rudy was sitting.

Noack then got up and walked over to thank Rudy and Fritz for an excellent job that night. He noticed that Rudy was being treated for a blister. After thanking them, he told Rudy, "Tonight after we get to position three, which is only an hour or so away, you can set up the guard shifts and rest all night. I will be going with Ernst and Fritz to position one to finalize our plan of attack on the bridge."

Rudy smiled and thanked his Commander as did Fritz.

Ernst wasn't resting but standing guard duty while Hans

treated Rudy. Noack said, "As soon as Hans is done, you get some rest. Give me the machine pistol. I'll stand guard until the next shift starts. You men, including Hans, need rest."

"Yes, sir, thank you."

Ernst went out and sat with the others until Hans finished. Hans headed for the medic culvert, got into his sleeping bag, and was quickly asleep. Rudy, Ernst, and Fritz, feeling good that Oberleutnant Noack was pleased with their report, got into their sleeping bags, too. Noack walked around the deserted construction site, keeping a close eye on the mostly overgrown temporary road in and back out of the abandoned construction site. He thought of World War I and walking guard as an adolescent in 1918 when they were about to move out to try to retake territory the Reichswehr had lost in a prior battle in 1917 against British troops. He thought, "How stupid was that on both sides. Many young men were killed in 1917, and as it turned out, even though we got our ground back in the Spring of 1918, even more young men on both sides died. Many families of German and Allied nations were changed forever, and then in a matter of months we surrendered and Belgium got the territory back again."

As he walked, he looked around. Fritz came up and said, "Sir, time for my shift," and saluted. Noack returned the salute silently and walked toward his culvert. He laid in his sleeping bag thinking of friends he had lost in World War I and fell asleep.

While the Commander slept, Ernst woke about 1500 hours and decided he would add thirty minutes to everyone's guard shift so the Commander could sleep until time for Hans to check their feet. About 1730 hours Hans gently woke Noack, who said, "Damn, did I oversleep, Hans?" Hans replied, "No, Herr Oberleutnant. The Stabsfeldwebel changed the guard shifts." Noack responded, "I see. I guess it's time for my feet." "Yes, sir, it is," he replied.

They followed the usual routine, and Hans and the Commander went over for full rations and milk. Rudy was on guard and had already eaten. When all had finished, they used the slit trench, covered it, and threw some brush over the disturbed dirt, gathered all gear and moved out toward their next camp, position three. It was only an hour or so away, and the weather report was right so far. The temperature was definitely dropping. Light snow started after they had been on the move for about twenty minutes. They had moved out at 1930 hours with Fritz knowing the route well, only about one hundred yards ahead of the single file, Ernst was ahead about fifty yards, and Rudy was bringing up the rear.

They arrived at the spot to leave the trail into the dense area with a dell and high brush. No need to rake their footprints into the area, they would be covered by snow within minutes. Noack and his team fell into their routines and they had the camp set up at 2230 hours. Rudy and Hans would rotate on guard on three hour shifts while Noack, Ernst, and Fritz went to positions two and one for the Commander's observation of the bridge and petrol tanks, and then the Commander would make the final decision on the attack.

Noack and his team moved out toward the positions and Šabac . They left at 2315 hours. All was undisturbed at position two, so they moved on to position one. It was cold with light snow at 0020 hours when they arrived. Noack looked through his binoculars at both ends of the empty bridge. As Private Thomsen had described, both guard shacks had coal smoke pouring out of their chimneys. He could also see the petrol storage tanks with one very close to the bridge and a two lane road leading onto the bridge on the eastern side. It would indeed be easy, he thought, "for young Fritz to row across in moderate snow and poor visibility. In our white camo we will again be almost invisible. It's an easy dash up alongside next to the entrance to the bridge. It's on the opposite side of the guard shack, fire the Panzerfaust and get back to the boat and row to us. Damn good plan."

Noack smiled at Fritz and Ernst and told Ernst, "Your plan is approved with my compliments."

Ernst smiled, "May I explain to Fritz?"

"Yes, of course. Let's walk down single file on that animal trail to the farm road. There isn't anyone in sight anywhere and in white it should be safe."

After five minutes or so the three went downhill to the path or trail and turned left down the gentle slope to the farm road which goes to the bridge. Ernst watched the rear and Fritz the front. They walked about two hundred yards closer in the falling snow, which was beginning to pile up nicely. They turned around, not worrying about their trail, which would disappear rapidly.

They arrived back at position three, their camp. It was 0330. Ernst and Noack went to sleep in their sleeping bags with their ponchos over and under. Fritz relieved the guard.

The usual routines in a Noack operation were maintained until 1600 hours when the guard told Ernst everything was clear. In the light snow, which was beginning to thicken as the temperature was hovering just about freezing, visibility was decreasing. Ernst decided to wake the Commander and Rudy so they could go over their plans one last time before heading to the target in Šabac . Noack agreed while washing his hands and face with very cold water that Ernst had brought. Rudy joined them in a few minutes. The three looked at Ernst's sketches of the west side of the bridge and Noack asked, "How long will it take you and Rudy to set the charges and run the wire to the detonator?"

He replied, "In this weather and visibility two hours tops if Rudy and I can get help from Fritz before he rows across to set up the diversion."

Noack responded, "Of course, whatever you need." Rudy agreed, stating that Fritz would be great help using hand signals to them from under the bridge as they were climbing around the critical places for the charges. Also, when in place, they could drop the ends of the wires from set charges to Fritz, who could bundle them and cover them on the way out to the detonator. After they had inspected all connections to the charges, they would climb down and join Oberleutnant Noack and Fritz at the detonator. It would be hidden in large, snow covered hedges just out from the bridge toward position one. Ernst would connect the wire to the detonator so all charges would blow at once.

Noack agreed that it all sounded workable if the weather didn't let up. He then stated, "After Fritz is in place on the east shore of the bridge, I'll signal him with one bird call. He will then climb the small rise from the shore and fire the Panzerfaust into the petrol tank closest to the bridge entrance and return to us. When he is with us again, Ernst, you will detonate the charges on my command. Understood?"

Both Ernst and Rudy nodded and said, "Klar, Herr Oberleutnant."

"Good. Go brief Fritz while I brief Hans. Also, I want everyone to wear two pairs of socks tonight. I'll tell Hans."

Ernst and Rudy nodded and left to wake Fritz. Noack walked over to Hans, who was back on guard duty, and told him about the socks and to start his foot procedure as soon as he was off guard. Noack then went over to Ernst, Rudy, and Fritz sitting under a low hanging poncho well under the snow covered high brush. He listened while the three discussed their plan of action once at the bridge. It sounds, he thought, "well thought out by Ernst, the senior demo man." Noack told them he was satisfied with their plan. Noack told Fritz, "Once you are back with us at the detonator, before we blow the bridge, go back to position one and help Hans with covering fire." Fritz responded, "Ja'wohl, Herr Oberleutnant."

Noack walked over to Hans on guard duty and reminded Hans when he was to be with the medical supplies at position one when they came running back. "Get out plenty of MP and rifle ammo. You provide cover fire if we are being pursued by Partisans or anyone. Hans, you and Fritz fire the MP's and the rifle from different positions and the sidearm from a third position so they will think there is a squad or more covering for us. When we are close enough to you, throw grenades over us to their positions. Once we are in with you and treated if necessary, you and Fritz will fall back to position two. Ernst and I will provide cover while Rudy follows you. After Rudy has had a good start, Ernst and I will throw more grenades down on them and spray two machine pistols at them. Then we will run toward position two with the three of you providing covering fire for us. Understood?"

Hans responded by nodding in the affirmative.

Then Noack walked over to the demo team and Fritz.

Noack then told Ernst to have Fritz relieve Hans on guard so he can start inspecting and treating feet and issuing socks. He said,

"Rudy, get the rations ready as soon as Hans finishes with you. With this heavier snow I want to move out early. No one will see us." Rudy responded, "Ja'wohl, Herr Oberleutnant."

Noack left to have some private time to think over each step one more time.

Hans finally got to the Commander for his foot inspection. Noack told him, "Hans, please insert a piece of thick cardboard under the hole in my boot near my little toe and give me the two pairs of socks." Hans said, "Yes, sir," and continued. When finished, he and the Commander walked over for their rations.

Ernst had finished and relieved Fritz on guard as Rudy walked over and asked for the time to break camp. It was 1650. Noack replied, "Tell Ernst to go ahead and start breaking camp now. We move out at 1730."

"Ja'wohl, Herr Oberleutnant."

At 1730 Fritz took the point out about ten yards in moderate snow. Then a column of men in single file, Ernst, Noack, Hans, and Rudy on rear guard. They followed each other's steps, only Ernst had trouble finding Fritz's steps, but it didn't matter as he knew the way. It was good the snow was covering the fresh tracks quickly. It was a little slower, but they reached position two at 1845. After a brief rest and after Rudy and Ernst made sure they had everything they needed from items stored there, they left for position one at 1930. As they moved toward Šabac , the town lights were not visible through the snow, but they could see a faint glow where the town was. All five were at their deep position one by 2000 hours. They knew they had a long night ahead of them. They sat and rested, grateful for the white helmet covers and white hoods pulled tight around their forehead and chin under the helmets providing some warmth. It wasn't cold enough for face masks, only about thirty degrees Fahrenheit. Noack told Ernst to find a stick or limb about two feet long and make one end of it sharp with his knife. He went on, "The way this snow is falling we will never find the animal trail back to our position. When we get down to the farm road, push the stick deep so it stands above the snow in the trail and throw it across the road when we return."

Ernst replied, "Ja'wohl, Herr Oberleutnant."

Noack then spoke with Hans, telling him again that Fritz would be back first to provide covering fire with a machine pistol. Keep him supplied with magazines and every few minutes, fire the rifle into their group from the opposite end of the ditch, and then fire your sidearm from the middle of the ditch, supplying magazines comes first! Noack knew that Fritz would have his medical supplies ready. He then stated, "We will take over cover fire as you head to position two. Rudy will be right behind you." Hans looked concerned, so Noack added, "Don't worry about being a medic firing weapons. We aren't fighting regulars. We are fighting Partisans and they do not observe rules. Regulars on both sides observe the rules about medics but these SOBs don't. Understand, Hans?"

"Yes, sir, thanks."

After Ernst checked things again, Fritz grabbed the ropes and wire. Rudy took the detonator and his pack full of explosives. Ernst had the rest, Noack carrying one of the machine pistols and a pack full of clips, several thick bandages, tape, morphine and the

Panzerfaust. Hans was staying at position one.

With a slight wind and moderate snowfall, the four left at 2100 hours. They made their way down the front of the ditch to the snow covered trail leading down to the road. Ernst drove the sharpened limb into the dirt at the road's edge. They turned right and Fritz led the men single file to the hedges where the detonator would be set up and where Noack would wait. He would observe the other side with his binoculars when possible, during the short breaks of ten to twenty seconds in the snow. They didn't hear any traffic or any people doing anything. Evidently people were staying indoors and the two bridge guards were stoking their coal stoves and probably snacking comfortably. When the wind shifted, the four could smell the distinctive coal smoke.

Fritz went along the shore and picked the lightest rowboat. He then borrowed two better oars out of another rowboat. He pulled it under the bridge and turned it facing the eastern shore. He pulled it halfway out of the water and returned to the hedges. Noack motioned for him to come over to him. Noack said in a whisper,

"Fritz, after you blow that petrol tank, bring the firing mechanism to the boat and drop it in the Sava midway."

Fritz responded, "Ja'wohl, Herr Oberleutnant."

Noack added, "Stay far enough back so you don't get burned and get your ass back here damn quick."

Fritz broke into a boyish grin, saying, "Thank you, sir. I will."

If the weather report was accurate, Noack planned to start the diversion on the east side several minutes before they dropped the west side of the bridge into the Sava. It would take less than five or six minutes for Fritz to get back to the hedges. If he heard gunfire over there or they didn't see a rowboat approaching in ten minutes, they would go ahead and blow the bridge. If Fritz survived, he knew how to get back to position one on his own.

Ernst, Rudy, and Fritz took the explosives, ropes, wire, tools, and white colored tape under the bridge at 2145 hours. Ernst and Rudy took the explosives to the underside of the bridge first. Rudy observed the Belgrade side of the bridge while Ernst was setting the charges on the west side. After two trips to the bridge key supports, they came down and rested for a few minutes. They then took wire which unrolled from spools Fritz held. Both climbed back up to the girders and strong pipes they used to crawl around on. Both went to the explosives in place and connected the wire to the devices on the explosives. This also took two trips and the wires had to be taped to the superstructure from the explosives to the end of the bridge above the place where Fritz and the spools were. They climbed down for the last time at 0115 hours. It had taken longer than they had thought, but Noack had counted on that. Ernst and Rudy carefully put all the wires together and put tape around them every four feet until it reached into the hedges to the detonator. After another twenty minutes of cutting and placing the wires correctly into the German detonator, all was set. Noack was confident that Fritz knew exactly where the petrol tank was and how to get there and back. He stated, "All is ready."

He whispered to Fritz, "I hope you can hear one bird call across the river," to which Fritz replied, "I will, sir. The sound will carry and I have excellent hearing."

"All right. If you don't hear it, use your own discretion. If you think you can do it and get back, go for it." Whether you hear the bird call or not, do not row under the bridge. To avoid flying debris in case we have to detonate the charges before we see you, you should, on arrival on the eastern shore, walk your boat down toward the Drina about sixty to seventy yards. When you return and row out, the current will grab you and make it easier to steer in where we are. Understand?"

"Absolutely, sir."

The four sat in the frosty hedges talking for about an hour. Ernst enjoyed his chewing tobacco and smiled when he spit behind him. No need to cover as Mother Nature was doing an adequate job.

Noack was briefing the three NCOs on news he hadn't shared from his last briefing by the Brigade Major. The Major reported that Berlin Abwehr (Intelligence) had estimated that Wehrmacht units had twenty thousand casualties from Belgrade and from our other units in Yugoslavia, including the 22nd Division run through to rescue trapped Kameraden. Berlin also said twelve thousand escaped over this bridge. Private Thomsen says it was a lot less. He reported thousands lay wounded and dead along the road from Belgrade. With Ernst's translation of the Bolshevist newspaper, Tito claims that von Weichs' and Lohr's army groups were really chewed up. Tito estimated that we had one hundred thousand casualties. Noack stated, "Soviets are mopping up east of the Sava through Hungary to Austria, and Tito, his communist partisans, the Chetniks, and another former ally, the Bulgarian soldiers, will stay west of the Sava mopping up mostly on the western edge of Yugoslavia. To me, this means our casualties are probably somewhere between Berlin's and Tito's estimate, probably fifty to sixty thousand. It also means, for us heading to Austria after Sarajevo, that the central area is the safest for us. We must stay roughly five miles inland from the Sava on our right all the way. We will zig-zag around that five mile distance, keeping a close eye out for Ivan's scouts approaching us from the river and Tito's recon men from our left. Our two recon men should observe both areas from a good distance, focusing on our left and right sides as we move north to safety. Understood?"

The three NCOs nodded and whispered in unison, "Ja'wohl, Herr Oberleutnant."

Noack responded, "Good, because one of you men may become the commander of this little squad shortly. Now, gentlemen, it is time. Fritz, get to your rowboat and make us proud."

Fritz stood, quickly saluted and grabbed the Panzerfaust while Noack returned the salute while seated. Fritz moved to the west shore and his small rowboat. Rowing with the current out into the middle where the current drops off, he rowed to a spot on the eastern shore under the middle of the bridge. Following the Oberleutnant's order, he walked north toward the Drina, pulling his light boat with him. The snow was coming down continually and visibility was very limited. He pulled the boat about fifty yards from the bridge up on the shore, pointing in the direction of where he thought hedges were on the western shore. Fritz made his way back under the bridge and waited for the bird call. It was 0322 hours. He had been gone about twelve minutes. It was not windy. The snow seemed to come straight down. Fritz heard one bird call and moved out with the Panzerfaust. He walked, slid, and crawled up the slightly slick embankment, thinking "tread on boots is important, wish I had some."

Thanks to a good employee at the petrol tank, a large safety light illuminated it. Noack, looking through his binoculars, couldn't see more than a few feet away in the snow. Fritz braced the anti-tank weapon on a fence post and aimed a little higher than the spot he had picked out earlier. He fired and, as it hit, he had already turned and was headed toward the incline. The blast was felt on his backside as he moved, and within seconds the whole area was lit up with a massive blaze, no need for grenades. He felt the heat as he was sliding down the incline to the shore. The fire was expanding toward the bridge and road and all buildings, cars, and brush that were in its path. Fritz didn't look back but went straight to his boat and pushed off as the snow fell nicely.

Noack, Ernst, and Rudy watched the big glow getting bigger and the bridge guard coming out above but not visible. He was letting the barrier down to prevent traffic from going onto the bridge.

Noack changed his view to the river's edge looking for Fritz, but visibility was too poor. They looked and waited. They heard small explosions across the Sava, probably some vehicles' gas tanks. They also heard women's voices and a few men up by the western bridge barrier, excited about the fire and the explosions across the river. Noack saw Fritz about five feet away headed right toward him. Noack was beaming and gave Fritz a big hug, saying, "Good job, Corporal Peiper."

Ernst and Rudy joined in and then knelt down rechecking the detonator. Noack looked at his watch. It was 0340 hours with total confusion on both sides. One second later Noack looked down and said, "Fire!" He then told Rudy, as the noise from the large explosion and the west end of the bridge falling into the Sava subsided, to go to Hans in position one and "be prepared to give covering fire over us as we come up that trail. Look for the stick. Go!" Rudy set off, double-timing it.

Noack then told Ernst to throw the German detonator in the Sava as far as he could. "Fritz and I will head toward position one. You catch up." Ernst immediately headed to the river with the detonator as Fritz and Noack headed toward position one with Noack favoring his left foot. They were almost to the erect stick when they heard someone behind them. They squatted down, and in a few seconds, Ernst could be seen. They stood and the three headed for the stick, staying close to the left side of the road in order not to miss it.

Ernst stopped and pointed to the snow piled stick. He then pulled it out and tossed it away. About four inches of snow had accumulated on the ground in our location. Ernst went first, making a clear path of footprints for them. Fritz was last, and to be safe he erased their footprints with piled up snow for three feet from the road. He then caught up with the slower Commander.

When they slid into the ditch, all exchanged greetings and Noack told Hans and Rudy to take medical supplies, extra ammo, and rations to position two. He, Fritz, and Ernst would stay covering their withdrawal.

"Go!"

After the three had watched down the hill toward Šabac ,
besides the glow and faint noises, they didn't see or hear anyone on
the road. Noack ordered, "Grab anything left that may be important
and let's get to position two." Ernst grabbed one rope that hadn't
been used or even taken to the bridge. The three left for position
two at 0410 hours.

While they walked single file toward position two, Noack's
usually focused mind wandered, first to his family who by now were
seeing Soviet incursions if not occupation in Cottbus. He hoped
they were safe and warm. He knew the Soviets wouldn't be able to
spare many troops for occupation as they were headed toward Berlin
according to the Major. His thoughts then switched to George
Washington's defeat of the Prussians. He had enjoyed telling other
officers in Kolding about the attack and how surprised they had
been with the story. He thought, "I wonder if old George watched
this attack inspired by his attack on the Prussian Regulars." He came

back to the moment when Ernst asked for the bird call. "We are here, sir," spoke Ernst in a low voice. Noack handed him the bird call. Ernst must have had more wind than either Fritz or himself as it was really loud. It startled Hans, who was pointing a Mauser in the direction of the small incoming trail. Rudy snickered as Hans jerked.

Within seconds the five were together again. The three sat while Rudy and Hans kept watch. After fifteen minutes with his eyes closed, Noack came wide awake and said, "The snow continues, and even though the sun will be up, visibility will be poor. We know the way; they don't. We shall go on to position three by 0600 hours. We will be able to sleep safely in that dell."

"Ernst and Rudy, fill your empty packs with ammo and rations and let's go."

Ernst asked, "What can we leave here?"

Noack responded while getting ready to march, "Leave the oats. Some family will have good fortune."

They moved out toward position three. Visibility off the trail on both sides was so limited that if they couldn't see, neither could the enemy.

Noack was close with his sense of time, only twelve minutes off, and they were safely in the dell at 0612. Rudy gave out guard shift times and four went to sleep in their sleeping bags with their poncho over and under. With their white face masks finally in use, they were totally covered with snow that was still falling but seemed to be getting lighter. The temperature hovered around thirty-two degrees Fahrenheit until noon and then rose to thirty-five degrees. Except for guard duty, everyone slept for at least six hours but in broken shifts.

At 1420 Noack was up and looking around. Ernst was on guard duty. Noack went over and told him he would relieve him, taking the machine pistol. He told Ernst to wake everyone, get Hans going on feet, and Rudy breaking out rations. "I want to move out earlier and stay out longer each day. After we cross the Drina we can relax a little. Tell Fritz to come see me after Hans finishes with him."

In about fifteen minutes Fritz arrived where Noack was standing just above the dell but only his white helmet was above the high brush. Even in light snow, the trail for people was too far away for clear visibility. Noack began talking to Fritz, telling him that after great stress like last night people tend to get careless. He said, "Fritz, you need to be really careful. Don't take unnecessary chances. Double check before making your moves and we will get to Visegrád safely. Understood?"

"Ja'wohl, Herr Oberleutnant."

Noack continued, "We will be going out earlier each day and stopping later. The more space between us and some angry Partisans the better. Also, when we get near that stream where we took the farmer's boat, steer us to the foot bridge through the wooded area, preferably before sun up. If we grab another boat going back, someone will figure out that we are the same people. If they have heard about the bridge, they might notify Šabac or Belgrade by phone. We don't need that."

He asked, "After we pass through the abandoned construction site, how fast can we make it to that stream?"

"Sir, what time are we moving out?"

Noack thought and responded, "We will move out by 1530. That should get us to the foot bridge by 0300 or so, after a short break, moving out again"

Fritz thought for a minute while Noack scanned the perimeter after hearing a faint noise. Nothing important. He moved back to Fritz and said, "What do you think, my good Jager?"

Fritz smiled and said, "Thank you, sir, for the compliment. I feel sure I can have us at the foot bridge by 0230 give or take."

"That's excellent."

The group moved out on schedule. Fritz had gone out ten minutes earlier, Ernst five minutes later and, as usual, then Noack and Hans with Rudy about two minutes behind as rear guard. They moved single file in the snowy footprints now getting a little slushy. They took a quick break after Hans ran forward and informed Ernst. Ernst took guard duty, slowly enjoying his chew. The snow had almost stopped, so he picked one spit stop and covered it before it was time to move out.

The temperature was beginning to drop a little but was still above freezing. Ernst moved out first, Noack and Hans another ten minutes later, and Rudy followed after another five minutes. By 1800 hours the snow stopped, but it was still overcast and gloomy. They walked on in the direction of the Drina, zigging and zagging behind Fritz and Ernst. About two hours later Noack sent Hans forward to tell Ernst to tell Fritz to stop in a place for twenty minutes and then he was to return to them. Within five minutes, Rudy appeared and found Noack and Hans sitting on a stump about five feet off the trail. Noack told him to rest, he would watch the perimeter. Since Fritz would be moving out in about twenty minutes, they could rest for about thirty minutes. After ten minutes, Hans returned and joined them.

With visibility only slightly limited at nighttime, Noack could follow the footprints easily. Noack told Rudy to follow about two minutes behind. He and Hans left on schedule. They slogged on in the slush until 0130 hours. Ernst came into sight a few feet in front of Noack and told them about ten minutes ahead Fritz laid a limb in the road and they were to turn left on a new trail that's going closer to the foot bridge. Ernst told Noack he would wait at the limb and left.

Noack and Hans were back on the march by 0135 with Rudy right with them until they found Ernst and the log. About 0150 they made the turn with Ernst running ahead but slowly and Rudy throwing the little log over into the brush. Noack told Rudy to stay about a minute behind. At 0225 Noack saw Ernst coming into clear view, directing them to turn right. Ernst followed Rudy down another trail. In a minute they saw Fritz waving to them from about ten feet ahead. There was a small clearing near the small animal trail.

Rudy stayed standing as guard. Fritz told Noack and the others they were about to come out of the woods very close to the foot bridge. They would be crossing it about 0300 hours single file and walking in front of houses to the barn and farm road. "We will be at least seventy-five yards from the houses, so in our white if anyone were looking out their windows at 0300 he would think he was seeing five ghosts walk in single file." The three men sitting smiled, and Hans spoke softly, "Or five crazy people wearing sheets." Even Noack chuckled.

At 0255 they walked quietly out of the woods and crossed the foot bridge like a column of ducks, turned in front of the houses and walked quietly to the farm road and headed northwest toward the Drina.

After this long march, Noack had told Fritz to find a safe spot to encamp by 0600. At 0530 Ernst came back and reported that they would turn left up ahead. He would wait at the new trail. Noack nodded and Ernst moved back out. About eight minutes out they arrived to a sitting Ernst. Everyone was exhausted, but Ernst popped up and saluted Noack as they approached. The Commander returned the salute and winked at Ernst. About one hundred yards off the animal trail was a small clearing surrounded by a dense stand of trees. They set up for the day. All usual routines were in effect. Noack turned it over to Ernst and went to sleep in his poncho/sleeping bag bed, sleeping like the dead. He was surprised when Hans touched his shoulder at 1300 hours, saying, "It's time, sir."

Noack looked at him while trying to wake up and said, "Time for what?"

"Your feet, sir, and then some food and milk."

Hans handed him a damp clean rag to wipe off his face and hands and then started with Noack's left foot. After some iodine and a small bandage and fresh socks were on, they went over for the rations Rudy had put out. Noack, eating slowly, leaned over and told Hans when he finished to have Fritz report to him while Ernst finished the rest of the details of breaking camp. Hans nodded and said, "Yes, sir."

Within three minutes Hans was on his way to get Fritz, who was looking at one of his maps. Fritz arrived and sat when Noack motioned for him to sit close, Fritz said, "You wanted me, sir?"

"Yes, Fritz," the Commander responded, telling him that going north and then cast close to the Drina he didn't want to get too close to Loznica as it might be a perfect place for an ambush. "Do you know the area well enough to make a wide berth around Loznica farther from the Drina?"

"Yes, sir."

"Can we then go well south of that town and then return closer to the Drina near Visegrád?"

Fritz responded, "I know the area well, sir. We can do that, but it will be another long march."

"Good," replied Noack. "Tell Ernst to break camp quickly. You stay closer about ten minutes."

"Ja'wohl, Herr Oberleutnant."

He rose, saluted, and headed to Ernst. Noack went back to his gear and was looking at the dangerous route again while estimating the time of arrival at the buried flare gun.

Fritz moved out at 1500 hours, Ernst at 1505, Noack and Hans at 1510, and Rudy at 1515. The Drina was to their right headed southwest, but Fritz kept them three or more miles away from the town headed toward Visegrád, which was below Loznica on the opposite side of the Drina. The small column zigged and zagged its way southwest, changing to small animal trails as they moved on. As they were moving steadily during an overcast, gray day but with a comfortable temperature, they were making good time. The only discomfort was boots with holes, and the cold snow mixed with mud was irritating to say the least. At 1900 hours they walked into Ernst, who reported to Noack that they were about four miles east of Loznica and would now be turning toward Visegrád and the buried flare gun. Ernst saluted and left to talk briefly with Fritz and then wait for the rest of the team. Noack and Hans left about five minutes after Ernst and Rudy back by one minute.

As the demo team moved closer to their pickup place, Otto back at their camp was preparing to move to Visegrád the next evening. They had been prepared for four nights for the pickup but no flare. He and the others wondered what had happened to their Kameraden. Except for their one perimeter guard, Willie, the rest had gone to sleep about 2400 hours. They had not seen a soul, only a few animals following their trail since Noack and the demo team left for Šabac.

At 0350 Ernst was waiting for them and, when he saw the Commander, he said, "Sir, we are here; just follow me." As Hans broke into a big smile, Noack said, "Thank you, Ernst."

They followed Ernst to where Fritz was digging out the container storing the flare gun. Noack spoke, "Fritz, you have earned the honor. Fire the flare." Fritz, grinning ear to ear, fired the flare high over the direction where the camp was. The guard on duty was PFC Max Berger, the back-up recon man. He saw the flare in the distance and shook Otto, pointing to the flare, saying, "They're here."

Otto got up immediately and the raft was ready, it still being pointed to the Drina. All four were up quickly and running with the raft and oars to the Drina. They put the raft in at the same spot that Fritz had marked with a rock. Otto took the raft by himself rowing to the current, then steering to a secluded spot up river on the enemy side. When all had climbed on board, Otto and Rudy rowed to the Visegrád shore. Noack told them to place the oars back in and shove it toward the current. The farther it floated up toward Loznica, the better.

After about two or three minutes exchanging hugs and

handshakes, Noack told Ernst to go to Visegrád and wake the Mayor, who was loyal to them. Noack told Ernst, "Ask him if he can get the small hotel near his house to get us five rooms with two beds and at least two or three bathrooms for two or three days. We also need a big breakfast and lunch and a late private supper with beer, wine, and Kognak. We also need a laundry or a person who can wash all our clothes. Also, Ernst, ask the Mayor to check the guest register and get the manager to tell any guests they don't know well or don't trust to move elsewhere as all rooms are rented for a family reunion after ten a.m. Tell him I have his currency and will pay cash for rooms, meals, and other services. If we don't see you back here by 0800 saying it can't be done, we will be at the outskirts of town by 1030. Ernst stood, smiling, saluted and said loudly, "Ja'wohl, Herr Oberleutnant." Ernst left, tired but double-timing it to Visegrád.

While waiting for but hoping that Ernst didn't return with bad news, the seven men listened to their Commander as he revealed the cover story for Visegrád. He said, "If anyone approaches us en route or while we are in Visegrád, we just finished a recon exercise.

Your division briefing officer instructed your commanding officer to stop after the exercise. I am to thank the Mayor, doctors, nurses, and citizens of Visegrád for all their help when our division came through before, during, and after Christmas. We will always be indebted to the people of Visegrád. Any questions?" They all silently nodded in the negative.

Noack then continued, "With our beards, if asked, we were out about eleven days, not enough time to have done what they will be interested in but long enough time to look as we do." He then told them the Senior NCO had been briefed before he was sent to town and said, "We all are on the same page."

Noack then at 0820 ordered, "Rudy, take a column of two into Visegrád. Keep your machine pistol ready to fire but under your white camo. Everyone else will have their weapon locked and loaded and slung over their shoulder. Otto, you will be in the rear with me, covering our back and perimeter views. Ernst will be waiting for us at the outskirts to brief me."

They moved toward a possible hot breakfast with good cheer

and smiles. They saw Ernst smoking a cigar sitting on a bench with a civilian. Noack recognized the Mayor and went forward, turning around and ordering Rudy to have the men take a short break, half on each side of the road with Otto on one side and him on the other.

Noack then approached the Mayor and shook his hand, thanking him for their previous visit at Christmastime and for any assistance he could provide now. The Mayor spoke German fluently and was very cordial. He told Oberleutnant Noack that the only two guests at the small hotel, two merchants from across the Drina who were regulars, were checking out after their breakfast anyway. They are on their way to Town Hall to see me. He said, "I told my staff to make them comfortable with coffee and I'd be there by 10:50 a.m."

Then the Mayor said, "Right now, Herr Oberleutnant, the hotel staff is putting up a 'Closed for Family Reunion' sign as usual for this type of event. Noack smiled and told him that he was very grateful. The Mayor told him that he had four doubles ready and one single for him. Once inside, all doors would be locked with an extra brace behind each door. There were two bathtubs, one at each end of the second floor. The hotel staff will wash and iron all the clothing. Then the Mayor told Noack, "Ernst said you left a sled in the woods. I will send my nephew with a horse and our large civilian truck to go bring it back and put it in our cellar. When your men have finished their breakfast, they can take turns bathing in a hot tub. You, sir, may use my tub in my small room I keep there for visiting dignitaries. Before you get some sleep, I'll get your shopping list for everyone and personally go get it after I finish with the two merchants." Noack, beaming, said "It's like being home. Thank you again, sir."

Noack waved at Rudy to bring the men, and the nine tired Kameraden walked with the Mayor through the quaint streets, then through the back door into the hotel, smelling the food from about twenty feet away.

Noack excused himself after thanking the hotel staff and the Mayor for their cooperation. Knowing that Ernst had eaten before that cigar, Noack told him to watch out both windows on guard while he and the others ate, and he could eat again as soon as the first man finished. Ernst smiled and said, "My pleasure, sir."

There was very little talking during a wonderful breakfast. Food was served by the Mayor's niece, Helga, who had worked there for about two years. Her brother, Heinrich, was the handyman but was busy taking the truck somewhere for her uncle. Helga's family was from Stuttgart, having moved there in 1935. She was sweet and attractive. Everyone knew without Noack saying a word that she was off limits. These fine people had helped them before and they knew what behavior was expected of them. Hans finished his meal first and relieved Ernst, who sat next to the Commander.

Helga brought out his meal. He thanked her and enjoyed his breakfast. The one brötchen and coffee he had before his cigar hadn't filled his empty stomach. After the rest of Noack's squad had finished, Helga brought out pencils and paper for each man to list toothpaste, shaving items, and other personal care items they needed. Noack told them also to put down their boot sizes. Since the garrison was not manned any longer, they didn't know why he wanted their sizes, but they complied.

Noack collected the slips of paper and added his slip. He said, "Except for Stabsfeldwebel Steiner and Willie, the rest of you go enjoy a bath. After that, stay in your room until our clothes arrive from the sled. Fritz and Max will have a room, Ernst and Rudy will have a room, Otto and Hans will share one, and Karl and Willie will have the one next to Otto. Questions?"

"None, sir," replied Ernst.

As Noack and Ernst eased back in the dining room, sipping coffee and enjoying their safe haven, Willie walked his pleasant guard post observing from both windows. Actually, he could sit on the stairs and observe through both windows which covered the entrance to the only two locked and braced doors.

Helga came back in to set up the lunch dishes, glasses, silverware, and linen napkins. She worked around Noack and Ernst asking with a pleasant smile if they would like anything else. Noack, looking at Ernst, asked, "Helga, would it be possible to get two coffees with a shot of Kognak in each?" Ernst smiled and nodded in the affirmative, and Helga replied, "Naturally, sir."

While she went to prepare their request, Willie stood up and spoke to both loudly, "The Mayor is coming to the back door alone." Noack ordered, "Open it and welcome him, then lock it back and brace it. He knows the way to the dining room. Just tell him where we are."

Willie responded, "Yes, sir."

The Mayor had sent his secretary over earlier and picked up the lists. Now he joined them with a large sack of supplies. He then peeked into the kitchen and told his niece he would have the same as Noack and Ernst were having "but not a word to your aunt." Helga smiled and replied, "Okay, Uncle."

The Mayor rejoined Noack and Ernst. They chatted while waiting for their drinks. Noack and Ernst assured the Mayor how much they appreciated both his help and that of the manager and his staff. During their conversation they could hear young men clowning around upstairs as each took his turn bathing and cleaning the tub for the next use. Noack opined with a smile as Helga set down the well laced coffee, "They are basically kids." The Mayor laughed, nodded his head, and said, "Yes, weren't we all?" Noack looked at Ernst and asked, "When were your born in Bad Vilbel?"

"Sir, I wasn't born there. I was born in 1917 in Dresden. My parents moved there when I was twelve and my sister was seven."

Noack quickly computed his age as twenty-eight and laughingly said, "Ernst, you are an old man compared to most of them."

"Yes, sir, that's a fact. I feel like I'm forty."

The Mayor chimed in, signaling for Helga, "Both of you wait until you feel like you're eighty, and I just turned sixty."

They all laughed. Helga delivered a second round of drinks and stated that she would be in the kitchen working, adding, "If needed, just ring the little bell on the table."

Before he had his second Kognak, Ernst explained to the Commander that with seven subordinates here there was no need for the Senior NCO to stand guard. Noack agreed absolutely. Later, after his third coffee, he explained to his Oberleutnant he was ready for his bath and a good nap before lunch. Noack understood as he, too, wanted to get into a hot tub soon.

After Ernst had gone upstairs and Hans had relieved Willie on guard, Noack and the Mayor talked business. He and the Mayor first dealt with boots. Mayor Klaus Brandt said that he could not get military boots as the garrison was empty, but he could get black hunting boots. Noack told him to get them, nine pairs with thick socks. As for the hotel manager, he asked, "If you could just pay the expenses, no profit, it will be fine."

Noack smiled and responded, "Please tell the manager that is a very generous offer, but they are being so good to us I prefer to pay the retail on everything. Once we report in, there will be no way to spend this type of currency, and I was told it was expendable; if we needed things on this exercise, use it."

"Well, that's wonderful," the Mayor said, "as this little hotel is having a hard financial time as most businesses here are." Mayor Klaus then told Noack, "Sir, I consider you a dignitary, so let me show you to the hotel's best room reserved for guests of our town."

Noack looked surprised but smiled and nodded.

After showing the Oberleutnant a very plush room with a huge private ornate bath, Klaus departed, leaving a happy but speechless Noack standing at the door. Klaus stopped, looked back, and said, "I will have boots delivered to my office, Auf Wiedersehen."

Noack's bath also included a shower, and he thought "This must be the way Generals live."

After a good bath and nap, each soldier, wrapped in a large white towel, found his set of civilian clothes and shoes Ernst and Rudy had picked up at division supply compliments of the Abwehr, which had flown them in from Berlin.

Otto was standing in his towel near Noack's door. He spoke, "Sir, it will be weird walking guard dressed like a Yugoslavian Partisan."

Noack responded, "Unteroffizier Schroeder, it will be weirder for me to command a Partisan group." They both laughed and took their clothes to their rooms and dressed for a late lunch.

Going down the stairs for a big German lunch, the Commander saw Karl on guard duty dressed in his civilian clothes and said in passing, "You look good, Karl. Keep your eyes on the approaches to the doors," as he patted him on the shoulders. Karl responded, "Yes, sir."

After their large hot lunch of deer steaks, French fries, two vegetables, and soup and salad or both, they drank hot tea or more coffee. Then Helga brought out a small glass of Jägermeister for each. This was to settle their stomachs after a huge lunch. Later that night they would have a light supper, soup and small sandwiches and something sweet if they liked.

After lunch, Ernst called the troop to attention and told them to be seated, Oberleutnant was going to critique their exercise performance. Noack was doing this to protect them and the civilians in case interrogated by either side later. He went on for an hour loud enough for the kitchen staff to hear as much or as little as they desired. He went over each man's performance and the group's performance, telling them that overall it was superior but there was room for improvement. He was recommending each for a promotion of one grade when he reported to Division Operations in a few days. In closing, the Oberleutnant looked straight into Hans' eyes and said, "Our medic has informed me that many of us need more attention to our feet that's beyond his supplies and training. Therefore, we will be staying a third day. Mayor Brandt will bring in a medical doctor and nurse here the morning of our third day after breakfast. They will examine and treat us. Afterward, the Mayor will present each of us with new black boots and two pairs of warm socks. I know they won't be Heer boots, but at this stage of the war, I don't think anyone will care what we are wearing out in the woods."

The men looked surprised but happy and appreciatively clapped.

"Now we shall all go to our rooms where you will find stationery and envelopes waiting for letters home."

Ernst then dismissed the group as Karl was relieved of guard duty.

Noack spoke first in a low voice, "Ernst, after we get back to Sarajevo and our Division, I'll have to report to the Brigade Major who gave us this mission and probably go with him to Division Operations in case his Superior has questions. Then the Major will debrief each of you."

"Yes, sir, I know the routine."

"It will not do me any good if you and the men speak well of me to the Major. Understand?"

Ernst thought for a second and said, "Yes, sir, I think so. The Major knows me well and has complimented me on my memory several times. As I recall the mission, sir, you were the strictest Officer I've served under. You relayed all information and orders for the men through me. You did not, even in close quarters in our camps, talk with anyone other than to reprimand them and me several times. You always told me that our seven men had room for improvement. I can assure you that all of the squad will remember it just that way, sir."

Noack, appearing relieved, said "That sounds accurate. I am

going to recommend you for a promotion to Hauptfeldwebel (Sgt/Major) but not to the Officer Corps as you are too close to the men."

Ernst responded with a big smile, "That really hurts, Herr Oberleutnant, but I'll accept that with gratitude."

They shook hands and had a Kognak together before going to their rooms for a nap.

After their light supper, the men went to the lobby area where the manager had set up several board games and two decks of cards. Three older NCOs played cards and the five younger ones played board games when not on guard duty or played music with the manager's records. Noack used the manager's officer to type up a report on the success of the mission and how the money from the expendable fund was spent. He also typed up the promotion list and honored Ernst and Rudy's wish not to be officers by asking for a one grade promotion for each man. Their mission's success would surely save the lives of many Heer and Waffen SS Disposition soldiers. Both had earned in his opinion as their Commander at least a one grade promotion or higher if Headquarters so desired. After writing a letter to Johanna and his children, Noack turned in for the night after soaking in his private bath.

The next morning as they were finishing a fine breakfast of eggs with bacon bits, brötchen with home churned butter and strawberry jam and, of course, several cups of coffee each, Mayor Brandt entered through the back door and sat next to Noack. The Mayor asked his niece for coffee and turned to the Commander as the men were headed back to the phonograph and manager's records and games. The Mayor, now on a first name basis with the Oberleutnant, said, "Kurt, I had some interesting phone calls last night. They all wanted to know who these Yugoslavian people were walking around in the closed hotel. Naturally, as a politician I had to protect my people, so I lied to them gracefully. I told them that you all were a very wealthy family from the other side of the Drina who wanted absolute privacy for a reunion to discuss financial matters without being recorded or reported to the Communist Party. They understood."

Noack laughed, "That's great, Klaus. Thank you so much." He went on, "Before I forget, if anyone from either side ever asks what I paid for rooms, meals, drinks, medical services, and boots, tell them I paid three hundred dollars in your currency, which wasn't enough, but it was all I had left. Then try to collect the difference if you can. This way I'm lying like a politician to help my men and my records will balance and you and the manager can make a bigger profit possibly."

Klaus responded, "Kurt, you have a deal," and they shook hands. Kurt also told the good mayor, "I'm going to leave our sled in your cellar when we leave on the fourth morning. You better dump it at the former Wehrmacht garrison or destroy it so the Partisans don't find it in your cellar."

"Good idea. Will do as soon as you leave."

Klaus then asked, "Kurt, how would you feel about tomorrow night having nine trustworthy young ladies come through the back door for the evening? They haven't seen anyone their age in about a year, since those damned Chetniks killed so many of our young men and your soldiers when they destroyed our railroad bridge. I'll come with them in a truck, and no one will see them come in through the back. What do you think?"

Kurt smiled and said, "I know what the boys will say but, Klaus, I'm so old compared to them and so worn out from our little exercise, not to mention I'm married with children. I'll approve it but will only be a passive chaperon with you. I'll enjoy seeing and talking with them while their date is on guard duty. You and I can enjoy that good Kognak and a female companion at our table while the kids dance and enjoy each other. It may be the last opportunity for some of them as I feel the next month will be more bitter combat against overwhelming forces and it's close to the end, but I didn't say that."

"And I didn't hear that, Kurt."

"Thank God for that."

Klaus went on and told the Oberleutnant that Helga would be taking the field uniforms home with her and she and her mother would mend them. He would bring them over in the afternoon and hold the boots and socks until then, "This way you can wear the civilian clothes until breakfast on the fourth day but have everything you need to look halfway decent in uniform when you leave."

Kurt responded, "Sounds fine. I'll tell the men about the dance after the medical folks check us out a day early. I know they will be very happy and even more appreciative if you and I can remember our twenties."

Klaus laughed and muttered, "Oh, I remember, but I can't do a damn thing about it."

Noack smiled broadly and replied, "Then you understand how tired I am after these days in the field trying to keep up with these kids. Maybe the doc can give me a shot to give me the energy to march back to Sarajevo."

"Kurt, I understand. I'm talking with the doctor tonight so I'll ask him to bring something to give you a boost."

"Thanks, and if we both survive this war, I will write you after I get home with our address as I'm sure it will change soon if it hasn't already."

Klaus thanked him and said he and his family will look forward to better days ahead and a visit whenever it is safe to travel. Klaus rose and told Kurt he had several meetings and a lot to arrange but would try to drop by for a drink after supper. As Klaus had the guard unlock and unbrace the back door, Kurt waved farewell.

Noack then went back to his room and soaked in a hot bathtub again. He took a nap before going down for the main meal, a large hot lunch. When he arrived at lunch, he was pleased to see that all eight of the men were clean shaven and had trimmed each other's hair fairly well. All looked presentable. They all enjoyed the meal Helga served cheerfully. They had schnitzel and French fries with two vegetables, salad or soup or both, coffee, tea, or beer. They ate and talked like civilians without a care except to satisfy their thirst for news about their Fatherland, especially their hometowns. They asked Heinrich and Helga to tell them anything they had read or heard about what was happening in Germany. It wasn't much, but every little bit helped them feel closer to home. The Mayor's niece and nephew were nice people their age. They truly enjoyed the civilian community.

After lunch and the Jägermeister, all went into the lobby except for the guard, who needed to be relieved to eat his lunch, and that was Rudy. Seeing this, Noack stayed at the table and had a second Jägermeister while Rudy was served and ate. This gave Noack a chance to tell Rudy, his third in command and the second demo man, how proud of him he was and confirm to him he had already typed up his request to promote him to Master/Sergeant (Stabsfeldwebel) on their return to Sarajevo.

Rudy smiled and said, "My family and I thank you, sir."

"No thanks needed. You men earned it the hard way," responded the Oberleutnant.

Rudy finished and excused himself. Noack spotted Ernst looking in and waved him over. He told Ernst that tomorrow before the medical staff came, "You and Rudy take all the packs down to the sled and fill them with all the ammo and rations they will hold. Get a large handbag from the manager and put all the grenades and the flare gun in it. Put the packs and handbag in your room's closet. Keep your room locked and get the manager to give you a lock and tools to attach the parts to the closet door. You keep one key and give the other key to me when you finish. Questions?"

"No, sir."

Noack then patted his stomach and said, "Take command. I'm going for my nap." Ernst laughed and said, "As you wish, sir."

Ernst, not feeling like playing cards again this early, went to find the manager and requested tools, a lock with two keys, and whatever else was needed to carry out his Commander's order. The manager took him down to the cellar where the sled was and he found what he needed. Ernst thanked him and headed to the room he shared with Rudy.

In the hallway he ran into Unteroffizier Otto Schroeder, who said he needed to talk with him. Ernst waved for him to come in and they sat down, Ernst on the edge of the bed and Otto in the one easy chair. "What is the matter," inquired Ernst, "You look tense."

"Well, to put it bluntly, Stabsfeldwebel, the men and I need to find some girls. Can you ask the Oberleutnant if we can get passes to leave the hotel?"

Ernst popped up in front of Otto, saying, "Are you crazy? I'm not going to ask a man who has already put his future on the line to get us this rest, with wonderful food and drink and new boots when many of our Kameraden are barefoot and starving! Tell the others to enjoy these comforts and show their respect to the Oberleutnant and the Mayor. They are both our friends."

Otto responded, "That's what I thought you would say, but I had to ask. You may be near thirty, but our four kids are eighteen and nineteen. I can't even remember that far back with all the shit we've been through. No hard feelings I hope."

Ernst replied, "None. Tell them gently, Otto." He smiled and left.

After supper all the men headed to the lobby for games and music. Noack stopped by with the Mayor and made the announcement, stating, "Men, the Mayor has arranged a great surprise for us tomorrow evening, but first let me announce a few things. Helga and her mother are sewing and patching our field uniforms tonight and the Mayor will bring them with our new black hunting boots after we get checked by a local doctor and nurses. I'm sure that you remember that they helped our division as we came through here at Christmas. We will change back into uniform before breakfast on our fourth morning. Also, tomorrow Ernst and Rudy will get your packs to load them with ammo and rations from the sled. Now, I will turn it over to Mayor Klaus. Mr. Mayor, you have the floor."

The Mayor opened with, "Thank you, Oberleutnant. Men, the citizens of Visegrád and I are deeply indebted to you and your officers for the countless hardships and dangers you have faced for your Fatherland and our town. I hope you won't mind, but tomorrow evening I'm bringing over eight young ladies, all over eighteen and eager to meet you."

There was clapping and cheering as Otto looked straight into Ernst's eyes. Ernst shrugged his shoulders and looked as astonished as the rest.

The Mayor went on, "Here are the rules. The Oberleutnant and I will serve as chaperones. We will entertain your dates as you take your turn on guard duty. We will not interfere with consensual behavior, but be discreet and private. No forcing anything. Is that fair and understood?"

All responded, "Yes, sir. Thank you"

Their smiles lit up the room. Except for the off limits Helga, some hadn't seen a girl or woman in over a year.

After the Mayor left and Noack retired to his room leaving Ernst in charge, they drank beer and sang German patriotic songs thinking about the beautiful Visegrád girl they would meet the next night. They were truly joyful for the first time since all of them left Crete except Private Thomsen who had been in Belgrade.

Most retired by 0100 hours, but Ernst and Rudy stayed up a while longer making sure the guard was sober enough to stay awake for three hours at which time Otto would relieve him. As usual, Hans proved to be reliable, so they retired about thirty minutes later.

Heinrich was cleaning up the lobby and setting the breakfast table as Hans walked from window to window every few minutes knowing now was the perfect time for an attack, but he also knew the Yugoslavian Communist Partisans were pretty lax and quit work early to "party." Heinrich left for home at 0230 and Hans relocked and braced the back door.

Otto appeared ten minutes early at 0250 for a chance to be briefed by Hans before he went to bed. All was in order. Otto took over and greeted Helga and the manager when they arrived at 0545. He made sure both doors were secure before briefing Willie at 0600.

As Willie made his short rounds while quickly drinking a cup of nice hot coffee brought to him by Helga, Noack came down the stairs. Helga had taken back Willie's cup when she saw Noack headed for the stairs. The Oberleutnant told Willie good morning and asked how it had been between 0300 and 0600. Willie stood at attention and reported, "All is in order, sir. No problems."

"Excellent, Willie. Let's hope that continues."

Of course, Otto had already informed the Commander. He just wanted to give Willie a chance to tell him if anything was bothering him. Privates don't get to talk with their commanding officer often.

About 0630 Willie and Noack could hear the others getting up, shaving and taking showers. By 0730 five were down taking a seat in the dining room. The Commander was already seated. He greeted his men and suggested let's just have coffee until the other two get down. We shall have a nice hot meal together. Karl and Otto came down and joined the others. At 0800 they began a traditional German breakfast. Willie stood his post with his mouth watering. With Ernst's nod of approval, Fritz, having finished his large breakfast and knowing Willie must be starving smelling the good German food and coffee aromas, excused himself and replaced Willie on guard duty. Willie thanked the Corporal and took his seat at that table that Ernst pointed to. Helga had already poured coffee and set down his first dish of food. Willie made the sign of the cross and said grace silently. He then ate his food slowly, savoring each bite. He thought of the many breakfasts with his parents and siblings, then said to himself, "these are my brothers now." As he ate, the others left after Ernst had asked, "Permission to leave, sir?" The Commander nodded in the affirmative as he had a forkful of apple strudel in his mouth. Willie and the Commander found themselves alone again.

Noack asked Willie to tell him about 19 October 1944, the day Belgrade fell.

Willie said, "Sir, I don't know if it was the nineteenth or the twentieth, but I was in the rear guard. It was a living hell. We were fighting Russians, Tito's troops, Communist Partisans, and at times even the damn Bulgarians. Seeing my friends fall dead next to me was horrible and just as horrible for the boys I didn't know."

Noack nodded, thinking of his boyhood friends killed in World War I and the teenage soldiers in Alsace.

Willie said he was one of the last to make it across the bridge at Šabac . He had been in the group that got lost in a bad wind and snow storm near the Drina. Noack nodded, remembering well when they were found and rescued.

He asked, "Willie, I know you're not an expert and probably

so busy firing from the Rear Guard that you couldn't pay much attention to details, but can you give me your honest opinion of how many of our troops got across the bridge?"

"Sir, my guess is about seven thousand. I know some officers estimated twelve thousand, but they went across the bridge way before me. On the road from Belgrade there were thousands lying dead or wounded on the sides of the road. I grabbed a machine pistol from a fallen officer and killed at least six Partisans going along bayoneting our wounded. Every time I saw a fallen officer I took his sidearm and MP ammo. I was firing three different weapons as we backed up to the bridge."

Noack told Willie that a few officers had survived and were in Sarajevo, saying he would try to find one, advise them of his heroic duty and urge them to put him in for the Iron Cross.

Willie thanked him and said, "Sir, I just want to get home."

"Me, too, Willie, but I'm still going to put you in for a promotion and find a Belgrade officer to tell him your story."

Willie asked if he could be excused.

"Of course, Private Thomsen and, Willie, it is an honor serving with you."

Willie, looking straight into Noack's eyes, replied, "Thank you, sir," and left. He went to his room and tried to put the retreat from Belgrade out of his mind. He took a nap, but his roommate had to shake him awake from a bad nightmare. This was quite common among soldiers on both sides except for the seven or eight percent of psychopaths and sociopaths who are in all countries, all professions, and all religions.

Noack also went to his room and tried to get the vivid images from World War I, Alsace, and the retreat Willie described out of his mind. After seeming like ten minutes, Ernst was knocking on his door, saying that lunch was ready and after lunch the men were going to help Helga and Heinrich decorate for the party until the medical team arrived. Noack thanked him and said he would be down in a few minutes.

After a festive main meal, everyone except the man on guard helped Helga and Heinrich decorate the lobby using the hotel's

Christmas ornaments and colored paper cut into stars. At about 1500 hours the medical staff had set up in the dining room. They apologized for not arriving in the morning, but they had an emergency that morning. They called each man to have his feet and legs checked for problems. Noack insisted they start with the lowest ranks first. That meant Willie was first up, Noack was last, Ernst was next to last, and so on. The medical providers gave everyone a clean bill of health and complimented Hans on his care and resupplied him with medications for feet and bandages for wounds. Noack and the Mayor thanked them and invited them to supper, but they said they were expected back at the hospital for a pending surgery. They waved goodbye to the men as they left. The men shouted thanks as they left through the back. The guard was right there to lock up.

Noack had Ernst call all into the dining room, including the guard. He told Ernst, "I'll take guard until the Mayor gets new boots and socks to all eight of you." About forty-five minutes later, all filed out, holding their new boots and socks, and headed to their rooms. Rudy relieved Noack so he could get his boots and socks.

They all came down and had a light supper with the Mayor and Commander. They ate quickly and went back to their rooms to get cleaned up for the dance. The Mayor and Kurt sat and sipped coffee. Kurt said, "Klaus, I don't know how we can ever repay you and your great citizens."

Klaus broke in and said, "My friend, you and your men and your whole outfit have prepaid for everything with your service to both our countries, and it is us who are indebted. Now let's have a wonderful party for these young folks."

Noack grabbed his arm and nodded in the affirmative. They moved into the nicely decorated lobby with soft romantic German songs playing on the phonograph. Heinrich's job was to keep the music going all night with the more than one hundred records the Mayor and manager owned. The lights in the room were colored by Helga in many different hues, making it look like a real party.

The moment finally arrived at 1930 hours when the guard unlocked the back door and the hotel manager and eight lovely young ladies came into the lobby where all the soldiers waited. The

Mayor introduced each young lady and Kurt introduced himself and the eight Heer soldiers. Ernst and Rudy, being married, had assured Noack that they would be happy to drink and talk, but that was it. Noack agreed and said, "Certainly, gentlemen, I understand. Just enjoy the night."

Heinrich began playing a popular German song, which was used internationally for slow dancing; the games began.

The Mayor signaled Helga to bring the Oberleutnant and him a bottle of Kognak and start the beer and wine service for the men and their guests.

As Klaus and Kurt drank and enjoyed the company of the girls who were with the guard on duty for one hour each, Ernst having changed the guard duty time so each man only missed a short duration of the party. As Noack and the Mayor talked with the young ladies, Helga assisted Ernst and Rudy erecting a beautiful large poster of a lake between the lobby and kitchen entrances. This made the entrance to the kitchen and the employee stairs to the second floor not visible from the Oberleutnant's table.

By 2130 the girls had picked their date for the night and the chaperones were more relaxed drinking Kognak and entertaining the guard's date than the young folks who were sipping beer or wine in between dances. By 2230 the couples could take off their footwear and be silent going up to the privacy of a hotel room. By 0230 six couples had taken advantage of this opportunity, never going more than two couples at a time so the dance floor remained full. As the party neared the end, they were all busy drinking and writing down the young ladies' addresses. The soldiers had no idea where they would be after Sarajevo so could only give their family's address and they were not even sure of that as the U.S. Army Air Corps had made millions homeless. They told their dates that their Commander had preached to them that, regardless of the outcome, their primary duty when they got home was to help the Fatherland rebuild. There was no time to feel sorry for themselves or stay drunk. Germany must rebuild and preserve the values that most citizens cherished, in religion, culture, music, art and, most importantly, family. They were proud to be part of this nine man squad. After a farewell kiss at the back door as their dates left and then climbed into the back of an enclosed truck. As they went by the Mayor and Oberleutnant, they thanked them for a wonderful evening. Helga and Heinrich were cleaning up the lobby and setting the dining table for breakfast. The hotel would reopen at 1300 hours after the "Yugoslavian reunion" was over and the soldiers had departed.

After breakfast, Klaus and Kurt went into the manager's officer and settled the bill while Ernst got the squad prepared to march.

Klaus had an itemized bill in case the young Major wanted one. The bill on hotel letterhead listed five rooms for three nights, three meals with beverages for nine men for three days and breakfast for nine on the fourth day, envelopes and stamps for letters home, and nine pair of hunting boots with socks. The total bill was equal to US currency of $578.50. Klaus told Kurt the bill included ten dollars each for Helga and Heinrich. Noack gave him $650.00 in their currency and told him to split the rest between Helga, Heinrich, and the manger with his sincere thanks, but the bill showing $578.50 less

$300.00 cash with a balance of $278.50 as they had agreed.

Noack had tried to pay the medical staff the day before, but they refused, stating that they were indebted to them.

Noack thanked Klaus again and asked him to purchase something nice for the doctor and the nurse, giving Klaus another $50.00 with instructions "to tell them it's from all of us." Klaus, accepting the money, said it would be his pleasure and he knew they would remember them for the rest of their lives. Kurt then asked for eight envelopes and asked Klaus to send Ernst in. They shook hands and Klaus left after motioning Ernst to go in the office.

Ernst stuck his head inside and asked, "You wanted me, sir?"

"Come in and shut the door. Take a seat. Ernst, this is off the record and I will deny it if it ever comes up."

"I understand, sir."

Noack told them that when the Major gave him $1,000.00 in Marks and $1,000.00 in local currency, he had told him his superior was so busy working on plans to go on the rescue mission south of Sarajevo, he just gave him the money, saying it was expendable and he didn't have time to waste on bureaucratic forms. The Major said he didn't sign for it and didn't want me to sign for it because it would track back to him.

He then said, "Ernst, I have $1,300.00 left. I'm keeping $200.00, $100.00 in Marks and $100.00 in local currency." He handed Ernst eight envelopes and the remaining $1,100.00 and said, "Divide the money up evenly among the eight of you but hold the envelopes until we leave Sarajevo. After we are a good day's march northeast headed to Austria, give it to them unless I tell you otherwise. Tell them we found it on a dead Chetnik Muslim Partisan on the way back to position one after blowing the bridge, and I didn't want any. Can you do that for me, Ernst?"

"No problem, sir. I am at your command now and forever, sir. To us, you're family."

Noack smiled and nodded in the affirmative.

Ernst asked, "Oberleutnant, what are you going to tell the Major so I'll know and we can back you up?"

Noack replied, "I'm going to tell him we used the money to

bribe half-drunk Yugoslavians. They were dirt poor and for money we got information about the bridge, traffic patterns, police patrols, military strengths, and positions near the bridge. We did this when you and Rudy did your recon with Fritz."

Ernst said, "Got it, and so will Rudy and Fritz. The rest won't know shit. What about Willie?"

Noack assured him that all the Major knew was that he was some kid who volunteered to go.

Ernst said, "That's good. Only the four of us will know that I paid for information when alone, and I'll let it come out in bullshit sessions at night to Rudy and Fritz."

Noack said, "The Major won't ask us about money because he will know how you got it and will prefer to forget about it."

Ernst responded, "Sir, only you and I know the facts and I will not tell anyone. I swear to Almighty God."

Noack shook his hand and said, "Put the envelopes away and get the men ready to get in the back of the hotel truck. Heinrich will take us out."

All nine piled into the back of the truck and were overwhelmed with the scent of eight different perfumes left over from their new friends. Several had left letters to the girls with Helga to mail for them.

After several minutes, Ernst spoke, "Sir, he is going north." The Commander stated, "I know I told him to take us north till we are out of sight from Visegrád."

The truck pulled over to the right and the men jumped out. They all shouted goodbye to Heinrich as he turned the truck around and headed back to the hotel. It would open back up in an hour or so. He was in a hurry as the manager and his uncle wanted to talk with them before guests and locals arrived.

Noack called Ernst about twenty feet away from the squad and gave him the marching orders. Noack ordered, "Ernst, have Fritz and Max alternate and lead us to Sarajevo off the main road, but on human paths off to the right of the road. Go nice and slow with breaks every hour on the hour. Smoking is permitted on the breaks. They can chew any time. Make sure cigarettes are field stripped. We wouldn't want a reprimand for leaving a mess, now would we?"

"Certainly not, sir."

"Gút, proceed."

Stabsfeldwebel Steiner called the group to attention with Noack behind him. He put Max out front with instruction as the Commander had ordered, and they followed after five minutes. The weather was dry, gray in appearance, but the temperature was in the forties. They had new boots and each soldier had a lunch packed by Helga in their packs on top of rations and ammo. What could be better? Of course, back in Visegrád with their dates, but that wasn't going to happen.

At the pace ordered by Oberleutnant Noack they arrived late in the afternoon three days later. They were at the outskirts of Sarajevo where the Brigades of the 22nd Division and Headquarters had been, but they weren't there. Noack told Ernst and the other seven, "Well, we beat them back. They must still be completing their last rescue of our Kameraden south of here." Then, to Ernst, "We will go into the Sarajevo Wehrmacht Heer garrison. You take the men to the consolidated mess hall and I'll report in to the Officer in Charge. I'll meet you there when I get our billeting arrangements."

About an hour later Noack arrived at the consolidated mess hall inside the garrison and found all of his men sitting at an outside set of tables smoking and talking. He motioned for Ernst and Rudy to join him. They walked about out into an interior yard protected from the streets of Sarajevo. They sat at one of the tables and he explained their situation. First, he gave them their billeting information and where to report and he told them where he would be and how to reach him if needed. Then he shocked them as much as he had been shocked when he reported to the Officer in Charge. He told them, "Men, the division got here twelve days ago with many wounded and left with new orders ten days ago. The OIC took me to the On Duty Operations Officer. He said that orders were changing every few hours. He recalled our young Major and said that our division was on foot headed for Austria and then to a train from near Graz to the western front to help stop the American advance. The Sarajevo Garrison and our wounded were waiting on orders to return also. Orders could come at any time. The Operations Officer said that a lot of rail track had been destroyed by the U.S. Army Air Corps, so we might be able to catch up with our division, or we could wait here and go with them. I told him I'd let Operations know in the morning when I turned in my report on our mission and my promotion recommendations." He told them they had a hell of a decision to make. He also told them that he had talked for a few minutes to an old friend who was a Hauptfeldwebel who had transferred here about six months ago. His friend had told him that the rumor was everyone here would be going to Berlin to assist in Berlin's defense against an expected massive attack by the Bolsheviki soon. He had recommended trying to catch our division waiting on a troop train near Graz. After a minute of thought, Noack continued, "I agree with him. Now, gentlemen, I need to know what you think."

Upon their agreement with him, he retorted, "Are you sure?"

"Ja'wohl, Herr Oberleutnant."

"So be it," Noack responded, "The die has been cast."

Both responded with, "What?"

"It's not important, just an old saying."

Noack then told them to get whatever they could for a long march, borrow or buy it.

"Ja'wohl, sir," they replied with a smile.

He then told them that the Operations Officer said there were about twenty of our young wounded ready to leave the hospital. They can walk and carry a rifle but will still be weak. "I'll tell Operations at 0800 hours, that Ernst, you will sign for them at 0930 hours. Rudy, you take Hans to the hospital supply at 0930 and let them get the supplies he will need for all of the walking wounded and us. I'll ask Operations to call down by 0900 to get the medical supplies ready. I'll sign all twenty-nine of us off the garrison and en route to join our division at 1330. This way all of you can eat a good meal together, see if you know any of them well enough to get information, and I will learn what I can with the officers at lunch. We will all meet out front on the parade field at 1315. Ernst, put the men in a small platoon formation, march them out the front gate with you on their left. I'll be in front at the right to deal with the gate guard. Questions?"

"No, sir."

"Okay. Have a good evening. Keep your ears open. I'll see you on the parade field at 1315 hours."

"Ja'wohl, Oberleutnant. Good evening, sir," responded Ernst.

Noack headed to the officer's billets to see if he knew any of the officers who would be there. Their names would be on their doors. He would also walk through all the offices looking for old contacts besides the Hauptsfeldwebel. He would then enjoy the large mid-day meal and walk around some more. After duty hours he would be a fixture at the Officer's Club sipping Kognak and listening more than talking. He had the feeling that he would never see an Officer's Club again whether they defended the Rhine against the Americans and Brits or Berlin against Ivan and his communist friends from many countries. So Noack sipped Kognak and appreciated the comradery of the Officers Club on 28 February

1945, wondering if he would ever see his wife, Johanna, or his children, Hans-Jürgen, now eleven, and little Hannelore Heidi, now almost four. Before last call for drinks, Noack recognized an old Stabsfeldwebel from his first unit, the 29th Infantry Regiment from the Guben area. He motioned to the old Stabsfeldwebel who, like Noack, was now an old First Lieutenant (Oberleutnant). He came over slowly, looking carefully at Noack, saying, "Kurt, is that you?"

"Ja, Martin, it's me."

"I see we have both moved up in the world."

"Ja, we sure have."

They toasted each other and talked of their time at the Guben Kaserne and their families that lived near Guben.

Martin asked, "If I remember right, you were born in Guben. Right?"

"That's right, but we were living in Cottbus in 1939 when we both reentered the Heer."

"Ja, I remember outrunning your ass in retraining."

Noack laughed and told Martin Schneider that he hadn't

heard from his family since September, 1944, before he left Crete for Athens. Martin told him that his family was near Cottbus and that as of last week all were fairly safe if women and children stayed indoors after 3:00 p.m.

Noack responded, "That's the best news I've had in months, Martin. Thank you."

Knowing Johanna, he knew that she was a strong woman and an early riser. He thought, "She will do what she had to do early with a neighbor watching the children. She will get back indoors with doors and windows closed and locked with shutters down before 3:00 p.m."

"Martin, I feel a lot better. My little unit, which will be about the size of a small platoon after we pick up twenty young walking wounded in the morning. We will be heading north behind our division which left ten days ago. We hope to catch up if their wait for a troop train is lengthy."

Schneider assured Noack that he didn't have to worry about that. "The U.S. Army Air Corps was bombing everywhere. Rails like our autobahns are a mess."

Noack told him as they finished their last drink, "Maybe I can meet you for breakfast and lunch before we leave at 1330."

"Absolutely. I'll wait for you in front of the Officer's Dining Hall."

"Great."

They walked out and toward the Officer's Quarters. Martin was first and Noack was in a building for officers in transit.

The next morning at 0715 they met and enjoyed a hearty breakfast together. They talked over friends and shared information for families if only one of them eventually got home.

They left the Officer's dining room and stepped outside. Martin spoke in a low voice and said, "Kurt, a good friend told me at 0630 that Operations told him they were expecting orders from Berlin early this afternoon. All men and officers are to be held here and reassigned to us and go with us in twenty-four hours to Berlin."

"Thank you, Martin. You're a good friend. I'm going to skip lunch. You last saw me at breakfast and don't know where I am."

"Absolutely. Good luck."

Noack hurried over to the enlisted and NCO mess hall. He spotted Ernst and said, "Get Rudy and Fritz. Go get the supplies now and meet me on the parade field at 1100 hours. Do not inform the men until 1050 hours, then move them to the parade field. I'll handle the gate guard if he tries to stop us. Understood?"

"Ja'wohl, sir."

Noack stayed away from the transit area and wandered over to the motor pool, acting very interested in the five ton trucks used mainly for moving ammo and other cargo. On close examination you could tell they were not made in Germany but by another nation and shipped in through Switzerland. Then German fenders and the Wehrmacht markings were placed on them. Also, an American oil company sold oil to a Swiss company, who then sold it to us. His inspection of the trucks and talks with the mechanics confirmed the suspicions he had since running the Wehrmacht Supply and Transportation Company in Colmar, France, back in 1941 after the French surrender.

NOACK'S MAP OF OPERATIONS
1944 SEPTEMBER TO 10 MAY 1945

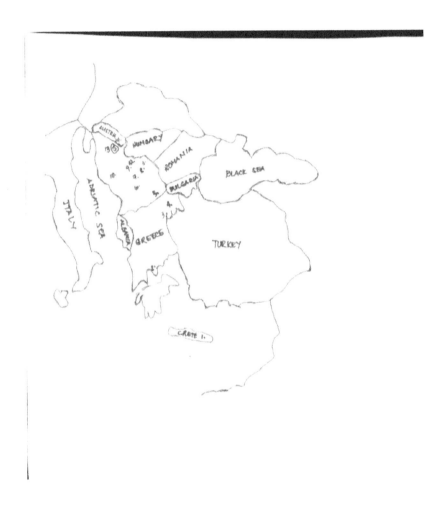

22nd INFANTRY DIVISION ROUTE MAP
SEPTEMBER 1944 TO JANUARY 1945:
Noack's Route
January 1945 to May 1945

1. Crete: Noack was assigned to the 22nd Infantry Division as a legal officer; Division alerted in September 1944 to move to Athens. All heavy equipment and weapons, and most personal belongings, left in Crete.

2. Athens: 22nd Infantry Division lands, transported by Luftwaffe Air Transport. Order to Thessaloniki by train at end of month.

3. Thessaloniki: After a few days' rest and reorganization.

4. Kilkis: The 22nd Infantry Division encamped southeast of Kilkis awaiting orders to march into Yugoslavia on a rescue mission of entrapped Heer and Disposition troops in three areas of Yugoslavia and then proceed to Sarajevo with their rescued men.

5. Dojransko: Unplanned engagement with Tito's forces, Partisans, and Bulgarian troops near lake, broke off, and moved to Skopje.

6. Skopje: First rescue of Heer and Disposition troops; troops not needed in the battles kept moving slowly toward the next site, engaged brigades caught up with rescued troops, supplies and ammo; all surplus destroyed to prevent enemy use, November 1944.

7. Prishtina: The second mission target, unneeded troops again kept moving slowly while engaged brigade freed Wehrmacht Heer and Disposition troops with supplies and ammo after the battle, caught up with main body of the Division moving toward the next mission target, Kragujevac, November 1944.

8. Kragujevac: Heavy bloody fighting, enemy reinforced from Tito's Belgrade forces, many casualties on both sides, rescued the remnant of the Wehrmacht troops, broke off engagement with large rear guard force using everything we had as we moved west by north quickly.

9. Visegrád: Crossed the Drina into this beautiful, safe town at night December 24, 1944. By the time Noack's battalion got there, it was late and the men could hear the wonderful Christmas music and see the festive lights as they moved to the encampment.

10. Sarajevo: After several days of rest and medical treatment of the wounded, the last units followed the main body toward Sarajevo and found the 22nd Division camped just east of Sarajevo and joined them; reporting in.

11. Šabac : After a misunderstanding with a young Major at Brigade Headquarters, Noack was made Commander of a squad to return to Yugoslavia to blow the bridge at Šabac . This would slow down any pursuit of the Wehrmacht troops' withdrawal toward Austria. As Noack and his men left to reenter Yugoslavia, the rest of the 22nd Division left for one more rescue mission of entrapped troops south of Sarajevo where the Drina meanders into enemy territory on both sides,

no longer a border.

12. Visegrád: After completing his mission in Šabac , Noack's squad crossed the Drina and sheltered for a few days at Visegrád, then on to Sarajevo to report mission results but the 22nd had returned and left, withdrawing toward Austria. Noack and his squad accepted twenty wounded Wehrmacht soldiers and they also left Sarajevo, hoping to catch up to the Division or at least to the American Forces rumored in Sarajevo to be in parts of Austria.

13. Ćelije Mountains: March and April, 1945, were spent on foot in ice and snow as they marched uphill in higher elevations into the Julian Alps. Noack used the Sava River Basin as his road map to Austria, zig-zagging all the way.

14. Somewhere between Ćelije and Graz, Austria: U.S. Army Forces were encamped. Noack and his small unit surrendered 10 May 1945, three days after the German unconditional surrender in France.

14

WITHDRAWAL TOWARD AUSTRIA, SURRENDER, BETRAYAL, TURNOVER, AND POW IN YUGOSLAVIA

By then it was 1030 hours. He turned and left and walked toward the parade field slowly. He sat at a table and pretended to be reading a letter of instruction. He had told Ernst, "Make them look sharp going through the gate. Once we are out of sight, slow down and see if anyone needs assistance. Do you have my gear?"

"Ja'wohl, Herr Oberleutnant," saluting the with Nazi Party salute. Noack returned the same. Ernst led the small platoon size group of men toward the gate with Noack out in front on the right.

At 1055 hours Oberleutnant and his small platoon sized unit reached the gate area. The crossing bars were up and barricades were being stacked at the roadside. The Senior NCO at the gate saw an Oberleutnant and a Senior NCO marching toward the gate. His orders did not go into effect for an hour and five minutes. Thinking they might be going out to pick up AWOLs, he motioned Noack on through, snapped to attention, and gave the Nazi Party salute, which Noack returned with his eyes right as he passed by. After clearing the Post and turning back toward the abandoned area where the 22nd Division had been encamped, Noack told Ernst to stop at a small park and let Hans see to any of the walking wounded who might need assistance. Hans gave out Bayer aspirin and rebandaged a few.

Noack, Ernst, and Rudy had a conference out of earshot. First Noack told Ernst that if we failed to catch our Division before Austria, "Forget the cover story for the Major. You and I got it off a dead Chetnik northwest of Šabac near Loznica. Understand?"

"Klar, Herr Oberleutnant."

Noack went on, "This is the first of March and our Division is eleven days ahead. Studying these sketches given to me in Operations, there are three main trails going north away from main roads to the Ćelje area. With all the zigging and zagging that our

Division is doing to avoid contact with enemies, they will be slowed down. This will improve our chance of catching up. However, the troop train which will be waiting for us, factoring in zigging and zagging between trails, is about six to seven hundred miles away. It is uphill all the way and rugged once we get to the foothills of the Ćelje Mountains. The nine of us have decent boots, but the wounded are almost barefoot now. Due to the rising elevation as we go forward, we will be in snow and ice even in March and early April if it takes that long. Tell Hans if you two spot any bodies we will stop and take their boots and anything that will help Hans care for us or enhance our mission to rejoin our Division. Questions?"

Ernst responded, "Sir, how will we know which trail to take?"

"Well, the Bolsheviki, if they cross the Sava (Sau) River, will follow the trail that was used by our Division. I'll leave it up to Fritz and Max to keep us on a trail near the trail our Division used. If we hear sniper fire or see any enemy coming from the Sava/Sau, it's Bolsheviki. If enemy or sniper fire is from the west, it's Yugoslavian Partisans. We keep moving but turn sharply in the opposite direction and then back north when Fritz or Max deems it safe. I will brief them tonight."

Noack continued, "Right now we have to get out of range of the Sarajevo Garrison or they may catch up and order us back. I saw a five ton ammo truck parked in front of the supply depot outside the airstrip off Post as we came to this park. Do you think you can get it started?"

"Ja'wohl, Herr Oberleutnant. No problem."

"Go get it. I'll have the men seated as if I'm giving them a class."

Ernst and Rudy stood at attention and saluted with the Heer salute. Noack stood at attention and returned the same salute, saying, "Good luck." Ernst and Rudy turned and left.

At 1320 hours, an hour and twenty minutes after the gates to the Sarajevo Garrison closed, Ernst and Rudy arrived at the park. Noack told Unteroffizier Schroeder to get them aboard now. As the men, with assistance from Otto, gladly climbed up, Noack asked, "How is the gas?"

"Full, sir," responded Rudy.

With Rudy driving, Ernst was in the middle and Noack by the passenger window to return any salutes if they pass Wehrmacht troops.

After an hour headed up the main road north, Noack instructed him to pull over and let the men relieve themselves and have a smoke. He also told Rudy to let Ernst drive and trade places with Fritz so he could show him the sketch of trails and possible enemy contact areas. Rudy carried out the order after the short break was over.

They were on their way north again. Fritz had many questions and Noack pointed to the Sava (Sau) River and then the trails, saying after today we would be traveling again at night and hiding in camps he found during the day in dells, ravines, or dense trees. Fritz understood.

About an hour before sundown as they passed civilian vehicles but not a single military vehicle, Nock told Ernst to find a safe turnoff to the left, northwestward, and then a dirt driveway to an empty lodge or cabin. They would stop in the driveway and Max or Fritz would make sure it was not occupied.

By dark Ernst had driven about three-quarters of a mile off the main road on a dirt road and was parked, letting Fritz and Max out before the cabin came into view. Fifteen minutes later Max came back and said a cabin and small barn were empty. Fritz was staying to check out the perimeter and routes by foot.

When they arrived in the front of the cabin, everyone unloaded. Noack told Ernst to put the ammo truck in the barn. He told Rudy to see how many people the cabin could sleep and to set up the guard roster with two guards at all times armed with two of the machine pistols with spare ammo.

Ernst came back after parking the truck, and Noack told him, "We will be here for twenty-four hours with two guards at all times. You and Rudy put all our normal routines in effect now."

"Ja'wohl, Herr Oberleutnant."

Rudy came out of the cabin and said that the cabin could handle eight. Noack told both of them to tell Hans to select the six most seriously wounded men to stay in the cabin with him. Noack and either Rudy or Ernst would stay in the cabin, the other in the barn in charge. Ernst immediately said he better stay in the barn to assist Unteroffizier Schroeder. Noack replied, "Good. Tell Max to go out and find Fritz. I want to brief both of them in the cabin as soon as they arrive back. Questions?"

"None, sir."

Ernst got most of the men, as two were out on recon, settled in the barn sitting on their sleeping bags. The two on guard had already taken their posts. While this was going on, Hans was getting the six wounded into the cabin for a check of their wounds and helping them set up their sleeping arrangements. Rudy and Noack's sleeping cots were upstairs on a large ledge-like structure.

Out at the barn along the backside facing the forest, Otto had his two faithful, Karl and Willie, digging the slit trench. The others were inside the barn eating their rations, half rations, of course, on the Noack plan.

Rudy asked Noack if he wanted the windows and door blacked out. Noack responded, "You're getting the ability to anticipate my orders. That's good."

"Yes, I am, sir."

Rudy took ponchos and hung and taped them over the windows as Hans tended to the young wounded soldiers. Rudy hung a wire across the entrance/exit (only one door) and hung a poncho the full length of the door. He then lit a candle on the small table in the open kitchen area. He also gave Hans a candle sitting on a small plate so he could see better as he moved from one patient to another.

Noack came down from his cot area with a handful of papers. He reminded Rudy to get Fritz and Max in to see him as soon as both were in camp. Noack went back to work studying the sketches and a map of the Sava (Sau) River Basin going north to the confluence of two streams that start the Sava in the Alps. As it flowed southeast downhill, it formed several borders . They would move north to the west of the Sava on one of three old trails away from frequently used roads.

Once they reached the area of Ćelje, they can turn sharply east and be very close to Graz. This is where the 22nd Division is ordered to board a troop train. While he was mulling this over and trying to compute a timetable estimating their ability to move forward going uphill into rugged terrain, he figured they could make six to eight miles per night barring extended combat or storms. He knew the higher they got, the more ice and snow would hamper their progress.

Suddenly Fritz and Max were standing at the table. Noack looked up and said, "Please be seated." Noack explained the route north and had them study the three parallel trails. He then told them that we would have Bolsheviki Recon men on our right, on the east side of the Sava, and the Yugoslavian Partisans and possibly Bulgarian soldiers and Chetnik Muslims on our left all the way. He figured that if they didn't see us, they would follow the trail left by our Division. Therefore, he wanted Fritz and Max to always avoid the Division's path. He also told them that if we took sniper fire from either direction to immediately cut in the opposite direction in a new trail. He told them not to come back, just drop local trash where we turn.

"The three of us have the sketches in our heads. Drop civilian trash and I will know where you're headed."

He also told them if they made the rate he expected, six to eight miles per day on average, it would be late April before they reunited with the Division's main body. He also reminded them that the nine of them had good boots but the twenty they picked up at Sarajevo did not. "If you spot any bodies, remember to take their boots and anything else we may need. If the bodies are German, take half of the ID for the Division and mark where the body is on my sketches when you come back in. If you are safe, bury our dead" He added, "Fritz, do you still have the bird call? I think I gave it back to you."

Fritz smiled and said, "Yes, sir, you did."

Noack smiled and said, "All is in order then. One toot and then come in as before."

"Yes, sir."

"Okay. You both get your rations and some rest. I want you to go out at sunup and find the trail for 1800 hours tomorrow."

They said, "Ja'wohl, Herr Oberleutnant," and went to get their rations in the barn and sack out.

Before Noack could get back to his planning, Hans appeared and interrupted his thoughts. He told the Commander, "Sir, it's a good thing that we put the six wounded seriously in here. One certainly was not fit to be among the walking wounded, sir."

"What is the problem?"

"Sir, he is bleeding internally. Something must have come undone on the march or when we had that bumpy ride in the back of the truck. When he is conscious, he is in good spirits and happy that each day he gets closer to home."

Noack looked concerned, as he was. He told Hans to go upstairs and look at the cots which are not more than a military cot and get Otto to help tear or saw the legs off about 1700 tomorrow and use as a stretcher for Private Eugen Geyer.

"Tell Otto to rotate two of our men to that duty every hour. He is to only use you if you are not busy with another person's condition."

"Yes, sir. I will do that now and then make my rounds again."

"Hans, let me know when Geyer is conscious and I'll go talk with him."

"Yes, sir."

Then he left for the barn to inform Otto of the Commander's order.

After eating his half rations, Noack got up to climb the ladder to the ledge where the two cots were. It was 2200 hours and he was exhausted. The Oberleutnant was on the second rung of the ladder when Hans came over. Hans had just finished his rounds and Geyer had been first and last. Noack looked down and asked, "Is he awake, Hans?"

"No, sir. He's gone. He died in his sleep peacefully with the Morphine I gave him two hours ago."

Noack came down and went to the table and sat. Hans followed. Noack told Hans to sit and asked, "You know what to do?"

"Yes, sir. Unfortunately, I've done it too often."

"Me, too," replied Noack, who went on to tell Hans to have Otto get a grave dug in the morning and wrap Eugen in several blankets.

"First, after you get our part of his ID, see if he has a home address in his personal effects. If he does, I'll write his parents from Division when we report in. Take his boots and anything else one of his Kameraden may need on the march north. And, Hans, one other thing. Please tell Ernst to have the wounded Chaplain Assistant to get in touch with Otto and hold a small funeral service by 1330 hours. Outline the grave with small rocks and a wooden cross. Hopefully the cabin owner is a Christian."

Hans said, "Yes, sir," and left for the barn again to change Otto's orders and to inform Ernst of the Commander's orders.

Back in the cabin Noack approached the ladder to his cot again and got up the ladder to bed. Ernst was now back in charge and Noack's routines were in full force as the Commander slept.

After Private Geyer's Christian service and burial, all went back to their assigned duties or for more rest as they would move out at 1800 hours after their half rations and powered milk or water. Rudy had them all refill their canteens prior to their 1800 hour departure time.

Fritz and Max got back from their sunup recon mission of the trail section. They had briefed Noack before the funeral and used their sleeping bags on Rudy and Noack's cots for a good nap. After they got up at 1520, they ate their rations and prepared to start the march. Noack wanted them closer. Fritz would leave at 1750 hours, Max at 1755, then Ernst, then Noack, then the group in single file with Otto as rear guard, and at 1800 Fritz, Ernst, and Otto with the machine pistols. Noack had his sidearm, the Walther P38, and the third set of binoculars which he shared with his Senior NCO; Fritz and Otto had the other two binoculars. Rudy had a sidearm and rifle. All others had their rifles, bayonets, and sidearms picked up in past engagements.

They were on a small trail closest to the Sava (Sau), about three miles or so to the west, and were making good time. When Max came running back to Ernst, he said Fritz had found a safe spot to hide as the sun was about to come up. "Look for civilian trash on the left side of the trail, pick up the trash and save it. March west about a quarter mile and he and Fritz would be there." Max turned around and went back to help Fritz establish the perimeter of the hiding place.

Ernst and Noack talked briefly while the men rested in place. They moved out after five minutes. Ernst found the trash and picked it up, directing everyone to turn right. After he saw Otto, he moved up the line.

It was a pleasant morning. Light was becoming more evident as they walked. Within a few minutes they saw Fritz and Max pacing off the area, selecting the places with the best visibility for the guard posts. It was a large dell surrounded with high brush for 360 degrees. Noack said to both Fritz and Max, "Well done."

They smiled and said, "With your permission, sir, we will do some scouting between 0100 and 0930 and report back."

Noack replied, "That will be fine." He then told Ernst, "You and Rudy know the routines, so take over. I need to have Hans look at my left foot. Then I am going to get some sleep."

Ernst responded, "Yes, sir. We will handle things. I'll send Hans over."

Noack left and found a nice place for his gear and sleeping bag below one of the two guard posts.

In the early morning hours, Fritz and Max went out to reconnoiter. About a mile north of their encampment they head several rifle shots coming from the area just west of the Sava. They moved closer and heard four or five more shots. Fritz thought, "It must be Soviet Recon searching for 22nd Division stragglers. Noack and Ernst also heard faint rifle fire and alerted all of the men. Fritz got within sight of the sound and saw a hunting party! He ordered Max back to their camp to brief the Commander. Fritz completed his recon and returned to the camp for much needed rest later.

Over the next three weeks they made good time heading northwest up the Sava River Basin area, zigging and zagging between rough, sometimes overgrown small trails. Fritz and Max did a great job staying away from roads with traffic and the trails that had been used by the 22nd Division headed to Austria. If the Division had used the east trail nearest to the Sava River, the small Noack group used the west trail, and if the division had used the west, they used the east with Max and Fritz keeping a keen eye on the east shore area at the head of the column, Ernst and Otto watching the rear and east and west, and Noack and Rudy watching for lights or movement by Bolsheviki at the center of the column. They were especially careful during sunrise. The sun was in their eyes when looking east, and the Bolsheviki were regulars, not poorly disciplined Yugoslavian Partisans. In fact, Oberleutnant Noack thought, "There might be some Brigades from Gagen's Fifty-Seventh Soviet Army mopping up through Hungary to the Austrian border." He cautioned everyone to keep looking east for Ivan and west for the Partisans. He wasn't too worried once they encamped as the Partisans drank and partied at night. Their camps could be easily seen with their big fires. On the east the Soviets tended to review progress and soldiers did maintenance and prepared for the next day if not on recon or guard duty.

Noack figured that they had saved about seventy miles of marching by borrowing the ammo truck, and they had averaged eight miles per night following Fritz or Max to their next dark camp. Noack figured they had come about 240 miles north, but now the gentle foothills were behind them. Their rate of forward movement slowed. They were now trying to climb mountains in the dark. There was no shortage of places to hide in the day though, plenty of gorges, dense forests, ravines, and empty shacks or cabins isolated far off the roads and animal trails. They made their best time just before sunup when they did not have to be concerned about the Partisans who were probably nursing hangovers, but Noack knew the Soviets, if in the area, would be up and have their recon teams out. After the scare from some hunters he was taking no chances.

While in camp during the day, two men were always on guard with machine pistols. Noack, Ernst, and Rudy went over basic hand to hand tactics with the nineteen walking wounded, and they had improved physically over the past weeks. All were reminded that, unless attacked, no gunfire. It would be an overwhelming response that they couldn't match. If anyone stumbled onto an enemy recon man, he would have to kill him or her as quietly as possible. If they were fired on, we would open up with every weapon we have, use the grenades, the machine pistols, and rifles. Ernst also cautioned them to keep their knives and bayonet sharpened and all weapons must be cleaned and oiled, if needed, and inspected before you slept.

With the mountains and extreme precautions in effect, they were making about four to five miles per night. Most was made at sunup and sundown. When possible they double-timed when there was adequate light and they had adequate terra firma, not on a ledge single file.

To complicate their situation, they were now getting higher day by day and the temperature was cold enough so the snow and ice was no longer melting.

Hans also worked with the nineteen who had worn out boots when they started each morning. He took blankets and cut the cloth to fit over their socks which would lessen the cold and abrasions from rocks and brush. He also used thin pieces of wool or cardboard to insert into their boots to cover holes in the soles. Hans did his foot inspections and treatment of each member of Noack's retreating platoon.

The usual routines continued throughout the last week of March and the first three weeks of April. Noack called for Ernst to take a walk while they were setting up camp. They went back about twenty yards and Noack helped Ernst spread his poncho on the ground. They both sat, physically fatigued to put it mildly. They were the two oldest men and Noack was nearly twice Ernst's age.

Noack stated, "Ernst, two matters we need to resolve as I have no idea when we will get to the Austrian border. I hope within a few more days, but no idea. First, do you still have any of those envelopes for our demo team?"

"Yes, sir."

"I think it best you go ahead and give the envelopes to the other seven team members. We don't know if and when we might be attacked and need to separate and be each man for himself moving toward the Austrian border."

"Yes, sir. I understand. I'll handle it tonight."

"Good. Ernst, just tell them we got it off that dead Chetnik and we both wanted to share it to give each of us a little money."

"Yes, sir, will do."

"The second problem is that Otto tells me that our rations will run out in a week, and I can't chance having starving men trying to move and, more probable than not, be in more combat. Please tell Rudy to help Otto start all of us on one-quarter rations this afternoon before we break camp, but let each man have eight ounces of powdered milk. We have plenty of that."

"Yes, sir. I'll get with Rudy and Otto as soon as we are finished, sir."

"We're done, Ernst. Get some rest."

When Hans finally got to Noack to inspect his feet, Noack told him that the original team understood, but Hans better explain to the nineteen added troops that we are going to quarter rations this afternoon. He said, "It is better having hungry men than starving men. We don't know how much longer it will be till we get to the area between Ćelje and Graz, maybe next week or maybe next month. I can't take a chance of our men not having at least some food with milk each day."

"I understand, sir. I'll see each of them now and then sleep some."

"Thank you, Hans."

Hans stood to salute and Noack waved him off, "I'm too tired to raise my hand, Hans."

Hans nodded and saluted anyway as he understood but respected his Commander and was grateful to be with him.

The slow, painful climb continued through April 1945 and into May.

On 10 May 1945 Fritz and Max came running back into their encampment about 0830 hours while doing their early morning recon for their route later that night. Fritz asked the Commander if he and Max could talk with him privately. Noack motioned to go back out the trail and he followed. Out of earshot, Noack asked, "What have you got, Fritz, a recon squad in front of us?"

"No, sir, the whole U.S. Army I think!"

"Me, too, sir," opined Max.

Noack asked, "How far out?"

"About four miles, sir."

"Can we get around them in any direction?"

"No, sir. We can backtrack and cross the Sava (Sau). We can try to enter Austria through Hungary, sir."

Noack told Max to go get Ernst and Rudy and send them here. You brief Otto and stay with him.

"Yes, sir," replied Max, saluting the traditional Army salute, which Noack returned. (Unless near unknown German officers, they always used the Army salute.)

While waiting for Ernst and Rudy, Fritz handed his Commander a pamphlet in German from the United States Army. Noack asked, "Where did you get this?"

"Sir, about two miles from their large camp the pamphlets are scattered east and west of our route."

"I see. Let's put down a couple of ponchos, and you describe what you saw while we wait."

"Sir, they have a large camp with a fenced off area with several hundred Heer prisoners, and their troops extend east and west as far as we could see with binoculars. It looks like they came in from Italy to their current position."

Noack said, "Damn, Fritz. We are so close to Austria it makes me heartsick," adding, "What does their pamphlet say?"

"Sir, it says we will be well treated, medical treatment will be rendered, hot food, clean clothing, showers, and we will be transported back to Germany to a POW camp."

"Well, we have a lot to discuss with Ernst and Rudy."

There was silence for a minute or two, but it seemed like an eternity to Fritz.

Ernst and Rudy appeared and Noack motioned them to sit down on the poncho. Noack opened up with, "Fritz tells me that we have arrived, but it's not the arrival we hoped for. It sounds like we have two brigades of U.S. Army troops blocking our way into Austria. They are offering decent treatment if we surrender and we will be taken by truck to a POW camp in our Fatherland. The second option is to wait. Ernst, did you get that little assignment completed yet?"

"Yes, sir, all is in order."

"Thank you, Ernst. Was it the Chetnik's left boot or right boot?"

"Right boot, sir."

"Ja, that is correct. Thanks. Now, our second option is to backtrack and cross the Sava into Hungary and try to get to Austria facing a Soviet force of unknown strength. Let me know what each of you think as my two Senior NCOs and my Senior Recon man. Fritz, you start first."

"Sir, I know we can't make it through or around the Yanks, and our men who are prisoners look like they aren't being mistreated. Through binoculars I could see them laughing and drinking coffee after sunup. The Americans were setting up a kitchen for their breakfast,. And I know what an SOB Ivan can be. With the terrain as it is and our current rate of travel and the fact that the Yanks notified their headquarters that they have captured Wehrmacht soldiers coming from Yugoslavia, I'd bet a month's pay that the American Headquarters notified all of their allies. Ivan will be primed and loaded to find and overwhelm us. I prefer to join our Kameraden in an American POW camp, sir."

"Okay, Fritz" said Noack, "Now, Ernst?"

"Well, sir, I trust Fritz's opinion about terrain and our chances. If we had two or three battalions of fully equipped infantry, I'd be in favor of a fast move through Hungary to Austria. In our current shape it would be suicide."

Noack asked, "Rudy, what are your thoughts?"

"Sir, I agree with Ernst, suicide."

Noack said, "Gentlemen, we think alike. Ernst, go tell the men to clean up as well as possible. Rudy, prepare a white flag that's on a pole at least four feet long. I will lead a column of twos with Rudy and Otto first with our white flag. All weapons will be hung over left shoulders pointing to the ground. Ernst, you will be to the left of the column keeping them in step and perhaps singing one of our marching songs when we get within earshot of the Yanks."

Ernst smiled and admired the order. He thought to himself, the old Hare is intelligent enough to know it's an impossible situation and is sparing our lives; yet he is proud enough to march us in like soldiers who did their best for their country. He responded, "Sir, I agree, and it has been an honor serving under you with Rudy and Fritz."

Noack said, "Thank you. No rush, but let's get ready to leave about 1700 hours. What is the date our war is ending?"

Ernst responded, "Sir, it's 10 May 1945."

Noack thought and said, "So be it. May God be with us."

THE SURRENDER

After Noack and his NCOs returned to the little camp, Noack asked the men to listen carefully. He spoke like a father to his young, inexperienced sons; only he had been a POW before in World War I. He told them that their war was over, but they would end it looking like soldiers as sharp as possible, heads high, in step, and singing one of their non-offensive but patriotic marching songs. He told them to dump any non-issued weapons and contraband in the slit trench and fill it in well, covering it with logs and brush. He told them that they would probably separate Officers from their men. He ordered, "Stay with your group and obey your NCOs. If they are separated, obey your senior enlisted man. If not, you will be alone or like an undisciplined mob, and that is not us!"

The Noack group broke camp for the last time at 1200 hours on 10 May 1945 and marched with pride, singing when Fritz gave them the signal with his damn bird call. The singing had several purposes thought out by Noack. The U.S. troops would know it wasn't an attack and perhaps take their fingers off their triggers. It would give his men a sense of pride as their war ended, and it might cheer up the men who were already in their enemy's custody.

Suddenly they marched into an area that had been cleared in all directions by the Yanks to give them a clear field of fire from front and both sides. Noack loudly told Ernst to halt the column with Otto holding the white flag high and clearly visible from all U.S. positions. They stood silently at attention like the proud soldiers they were. Within a minute, a young American Captain with a sidearm only walked toward them accompanied by a German Captain (Hauptmannn) who no longer was armed.

The American officer addressed Noack, "Lieutenant, I

understand more German than I speak, so I will ask Hauptmann Weichert to explain our procedures."

Noack responded, "Thank you, sir. I understand."

Hauptmannn Weichert spoke matter of factly. "Oberleutnant, you are three days late."

Noack looked puzzled and responded, "Sir?"

The Captain stated, "The war ended three days ago. We surrendered on 7 May 1945."

Noack asked, "Compiegne, sir?"

Hauptmann Weichert laughed and said, "No, I don't think General Eisenhower cared about our centuries old disagreement with France over Alsace."

When the American Captain heard the name of the Supreme Allied Commander being talked about, he asked for an explanation. Hauptmann Weichert explained politely, and the Captain laughed, too, and said to Noack, "He is all business, not much time for history. We all want to get home like you do."

Noack responded, "Yes, sir," and asked, "May I allow my

men to stand at ease?"

"Certainly."

Noack nodded to Ernst, who gave them the command, "At ease."

The Hauptmann then directed Noack to have his men one at a time walk over to a table on their left and turn in all their weapons. A clerk would record his name and unit and another U.S. soldier would empty out all the ammo and any other ammo from each man. Rifles will be stacked and then the men will move to the table at the right for his photo, and then they may sit in the clearing on the left until everyone is present.

He then said, "Oberleutnant, you and your NCOs will go to the table between the table on the left and the one in the center and give us your machine pistols and sidearms. No grenades?"

"None left, sir," responded Noack.

The American Captain reminded Hauptmann Weichert that the Camp Commander would talk with Noack at 1000 hours the next day. Between now and then, they can shower after delousing, get fresh clothes, eat a good meal, and rest up."

The Hauptmann explained the agenda to Noack as the American Captain walked over to Otto and accepted the white flag, returned Otto's salute, turned and walked back to the camp entrance as Noack and his small command fell into the routine as ordained by the U.S. Captain.

In addition to what the Captain had described, they were all given a pack of American cigarettes. To the men who smoked, it was like inhaling velvet compared to the very harsh tobacco in Bolsheviki cigarettes. Noack's men were not happy but at peace and got some much needed rest without worrying about being killed as they slept. In the morning they heard a bugle sounding reveille. They were all allowed to eat a hearty breakfast together. Afterwards, Noack cleaned up a little more for his interrogation by the Camp Commander at 1000 hours.

The Oberleutnant reported at the Camp Headquarters at 0955 hours and was told to be seated. At 1000 hours, precisely on time, he was shown into the Camp Commander's office. A man of his age, a

LTC, the Oberleutnant saluted and the LTC returned his salute and told him to be seated. The LTC had a clerk bring them both a cup of coffee. The LTC then asked everyone to leave and shut the door. Noack didn't know what to expect but was enjoying the hot coffee.

The LTC spoke first. "How is it you are my age and only a First Lieutenant?"

Noack responded in his best English that he had been a young enlisted man in World War I, and after the war became a policeman in the Weimar Republic long before the Third Reich. He went on to explain he went to law school and became a Magistrate. He also explained that he was recalled into the Wehrmacht Heer as a Master/Sergeant in 1939 and that he was married and had one child at that time, now two children. Noack stated, "The Wehrmacht sent me back to study military law in 1943. I was promoted to Oberleutnant on graduation and assigned to the 22nd Division as a legal officer, and here I am, sir."

Noack would not have given all this information, but the war was over. He hoped to obtain more for his men.

The American Camp Commander, in his southern accent, asked Noack if he had fought at Belgrade. "I heard it was a blood bath on both sides."

Noack responded, "I heard that, too, sir. I was a legal officer in Crete into September 1944. We went to Athens and later close to the Yugoslav border. It was around mid-October when we crossed into Yugoslavia and moved through the country enroute to Sarajevo, freeing trapped Wehrmacht soldiers along the way. We bogged down in heavy fighting south of Belgrade. We managed to break free and make it across the Drina to safety and Sarajevo."

The Camp Commander broke in and surprised Noack with the information he already had on their march from Sarajevo to this position, saying, "Oberleutnant Noack, to get nineteen out of twenty walking wounded young men here with a squad of eight is one hell of an accomplishment; I salute you. I am sure there will be many happy German parents and wives."

Noack was speechless but managed a nod and "Thank you, sir." As Noack was on his way out of the Commander's office he heard the Commander say loudly into his field phone, "It's all a SNAFU!" When Noack spoke with Ernst, he asked him, "What is a SNAFU?" Ernst responded, "Herr Oberleutnant, I have no idea."

THE BETRAYAL

The following morning Noack was recalled to the Camp Commander's office. The LTC advised him to be seated and "Have some coffee. I have some bad news."

"Oberleutnant Noack thought, "on the 8th and 9th of May this unit was doing precisely what is stated in the pamphlets scattered all over Yugoslavian and Italian terrain on the way to surrender." The Camp Commander asked, "You have read the pamphlet?"

"Yes, sir, twice."

The Camp Commander continued, "I am sorry and it's a crying shame, but my orders were changed yesterday afternoon by a direct order from SHAEF (Supreme Headquarters Allied Expeditionary Forces). Oberleutnant, I will not disobey the order."

He continued, "Off the record, it's probably the post-war politics from D.C. Your medic will be restocked with medical supplies after your lunch. Tell your men to eat hearty and fill their pockets with bread as I won't control your care after 1400 hours today."

Noack felt sick to his stomach, knowing what he had feared all along: he and his men becoming Russian (Soviet) or Tito's POWs.

Noack asked, "Sir, who are we being turned over to at 1400 hours?"

The Camp Commander offered another cup of coffee. Noack said, "Thank you, sir."

The LTC said, "You will be turned over to Tito's representatives who will arrive by trucks for their guards. You will be marched on the main roads headed down the Sava Basin into Yugoslavia."

"Will it just be us?"

"No, it's everyone we have here. They will pick up more

detained Wehrmacht soldiers along the way."

Noack asked, "Sir, do you know our final destination?"

"No. You know as much as I do now."

"Sir, may my men leave letters to their homes to be mailed from your unit to our families so they will know we are POWs?"

"Of course, Oberleutnant. I will get the word to all of the POWs that they can drop letters to home in a box before they leave our compound."

Noack thanked the Commander and asked for permission to speak to his men to explain the situation before their lunch.

"Certainly. I'll send the young Captain with you."

Noack stood and saluted, saying, "Thank you, sir, for your assistance with my men."

"You're welcome, and good luck. I'll walk with you until I see the Captain."

They left the Commander's office and the LTC sent for the Captain as Noack used the latrine. When he emerged from the latrine, the LTC offered a handshake and Noack shook his hand, then left with the Captain, who explained some information to the men assembled in the yard in front of the Commander's office. The Captain left complicated matters to Noack. When done, Noack advised them to wait with the Captain. The Captain would get Noack with an NCO who would take him and Hans to medical supplies to restock and then back to the unit while the rest stayed in place.

Prior to leaving, Oberleutnant Noack addressed his men, telling them to stock up on bread and crackers as he did not know when their next meal would be and to also write letters home and deposit them in a box at the gate as they departed at 1400 hours.

Ernst asked, "Where are we going, sir?"

Noack cut to the chase, replying "Yugoslavia."

His heart sank as he watched his men wilt in front of him. Noack spoke up, "It won't be as bad as our trip. The weather will be warmer. The Camp Commander thinks we will be marching on the main road along the Sava River Basin, and it's downhill all the way.

Their spirits lifted a little, but Noack knew they were hoping, like him, that they would be POWs in Germany. Noack continued, "We are alive. No one will be shooting at us, but we will get jeers along the road I'm sure, but jeers won't keep us from getting home eventually. Help each other and use your brain when responding to their authority. From what the LTC said, General Alfred Jodl and Admiral Friedeburg signed the unconditional surrender on 07 May 1945. We must abide by it."

Otto raised his hand. "Sir, why didn't the Feuhrer sign it? He may not agree?"

Noack responded, "The Fuehrer is dead. The war is over. We must accept this. We are released from any oaths or promises we made. We now only owe each other our loyalty until we get home. Let's go eat a good meal and then write home telling our loved ones that we survived and we will be POWs in Yugoslavia. I'm sure our new government will negotiate with Marshal Tito for our release as they will negotiate with other Allied nations for our Kameraden's releases. Keep your heads, obey your orders, help each other, and we will get home."

Noack then told Hans, "After you restock and eat, rejoin us to write your letter home. We must be in formation in the yard by 1330 hours."

THE TURNOVER TO YUGOSLAVIA

After their last full hot lunch for a long time to come, they were on their way to the tents they were assigned, Ernst asked Noack in private if he had been asked about the bridge. Noack said, "Not a single question. How about you and the others with direct knowledge?"

"Nothing, sir."

"Good. The nineteen know nothing. Only four have direct knowledge, five may have guesses, but we admit nothing. Spread the word one by one in private that we heard rumors in Sarajevo about some bridge being blown up and thought some of our Kameraden who had fought in Belgrade might have gone back and done it. When we broke out of Kragujevac, we moved as fast as possible to the Drina and Sarajevo. We never went back. We didn't give a damn about what was behind us."

"Yes, sir, got it. I will pass on to those who need to know."

"Thanks, Ernst. If they separate us, you are in command. Take care of them."

"I will, sir."

At 1330 with letters in their side pockets in their new POW clothing and new socks and new brogans, they stood at ease with Noack in front facing the Camp Commander's platform. At 1420 they were called to attention, and he told them to stand at ease. He then told them, "The trucks are delayed, but the staff officers have arrived. We will be calling out units in the order you surrendered. As you go out, there are barrels of fresh water with ladles. Drink if you want. Leave letters in the big box labeled U.S. Mail. We will post your mail in the morning. Good luck."

The Commander left the platform headed out to meet the Yugoslavian Commander and the staff officers.

The young Captain they had all met with the Wehrmacht Hauptmann appeared on the platform and called out the collection of small units and one battalion sized unit in the order they would be called. Noack's small sized unit and their number would be the last in the order of turnover. When called, their officer or Senior NCO would report to the desk and call each man to sign in and be issued a temporary ID card. The German Hauptmann repeated each statement of the American Captain in German. Also, he cautioned, "We are Prisoners of War; the Yugoslavian Commander has said any prisoner who loses his temporary ID card before he is issued his permanent ID card will be tried for destroying government property and will be given additional time to serve."

By the time that approximately five hundred plus soldiers had left the compound, Ernst was at the rear as Noack was in front of the last group to leave U.S. custody. It was 1700 hours. Noack saluted and called his men up to the tables one per session. When done, they fell in at the rear of a long formation, four across with Noack at the front on the right and Ernst in the rear on the left.

The German POWs were called to attention and they set out behind Yugoslavian guards, who generally changed shifts periodically and got in the back of their trucks to rest. The Senior officer and a driver were in an American Jeep with Yugoslavian markings running up and down the road looking at the formation.

There were only a few of Tito's officers. The guards were all the Communist Partisans. They all started southeast, following the route created by the Sava River. It was so much easier going downhill on a street than on animal trails going uphill with possible sniper fire. It cheered them a little. The snipers never injured any of Noack's men. Fritz just moved them in the opposite direction to another trail going northwest. Fritz had seen places where the main body of the 22nd Division had been engaged in small attacks going northwest, but they hadn't seen the places as they were always rerouted on alternate trails, thanks to Fritz or Max.

Even though it was an easier route, we moved very slowly after getting hot water and, if lucky, coffee made from old used grinds from the guards' coffee and stale bits of bread leftover from their last evening meal. Lunch was sugar water to give them energy and some type of hot cabbage or red beets. Supper was after the guards ate and was usually some concoction made into a stew with all their leftovers. We ate it to survive but looked back at our half rations with fondness.

We moved slowly not because of us but because the guards were in no hurry. As before, the Partisans quit early and set up their camps. They would have us use posthole diggers to set poles for barbed wire at about 1600 hours daily for an area just large enough for all of us to lie down with slit trenches at all four corners. Four armed guards walked between their posts. Then their campfires started and the alcohol flowed. We slept on the ground with one blanket each.

Our small unit stuck together, and Hans checked us whenever we had a complaint. Some of the other units still had their medics, too. They would come over and trade medical items depending on their men's needs. Occasionally all of them would get together in the area used by our group as they learned they could speak freely among themselves there.

The march toward Belgrade continued on at a snail's pace. Tito's few officers had left us to the Commander of the Yugoslavian

Communist Partisans on the morning of 13 May 1945. As long as we kept quiet and to ourselves and did what they ordered, they didn't pay much attention to us. Our large group was about five hundred men. Beside us, as best Ernst could find out, was about two hundred more from the 22nd Division who had not made it into Austria. No one really knew what had happened to the main body of the 22nd Division. The other three hundred plus were from bits and pieces of other units from the von Weichs' forces they had sent to form the Serbia Army Group.

As they moved toward Belgrade, Jeeps would stop the march and wait until other POWs could join our original five hundred. We picked up officers, NCOs, and enlisted below the rank of corporal. We grew in size by the week. The highest officer in the original group was a Colonel. Before other officers joined the group, the highest ranking officer had only weekly get togethers with all officers. As the Officer Corps grew, they met twice per week after the camp was set up and our captors were well into their lax behavior. We moved slowly but steadily forward in a southeast direction close to the Sava.

By the end of June, we had picked up another two hundred or so POWS, about fifty company grade officers, a few lower level field grade officers, NCOs, and enlisted. This included five Italian Company grade officers and two Italian NCOs. During the short informal officer meetings twice per week, the new officers passed on a rumor that all enlisted and most NCO's would be held at Novi Sad and officers would continue on toward Belgrade. Noack passed this information on to Ernst, his Senior NCO. If this happened, he would be in command of the men. They were ordered to stay in close touch, with daily conversations, after the camp was set up and the Partisans relaxed. Since the war was over, they had no duty to try to escape. Why get killed when the war was over? Noack instructed Ernst to keep them together, complying with their captors' demands. He told Ernst to explain to them they were not forgotten and that Noack knew in his heart that the new German government would get them out in time. There would be some kind of political consideration demanded and paid, then we would go home! Ernst understood and promised that he would do his best to keep them together and compliant until that time came.

By the beginning of July, 1945 AD, as they approached Novi Sad, they were getting a full eight to nine hours of daylight, and the temperature was comfortable with tolerable humidity. As predicted, on the outskirts of Novi Sad, the meandering group of POWs was halted. The NCOs and enlisted were ordered to leave the group and reassemble at a park on our right, while officers stood in place. The NCOs took over their small groups immediately and got them all in formation in the park.

The Partisan Commander walked over to the Wehrmacht Sgt/Major (Hauptfeldwebel) and instructed him to tell the group to be seated. They would be staying in Novi Sad. The Commander then turned and gave a signal for the officers to be started on their way. As the smaller group started off toward Belgrade, many of the NCOs and enlisted men shouted, "Good luck." They never saw these officers again until after the ones who survived were returned to their Fatherland for a price.

As they marched on, the officers could not help but recognize that the infrastructure of the county was in terrible condition and got worse as they moved southeast. The citizens were also impoverished.

By the end of July, they had picked up many more officers en route. They arrived at Vršac at the end of July 1945, AD. Evidently officers had been brought here from all over this theatre of operation. Noack had memorized the count as five thousand Wehrmacht officers, five hundred Austrian officers, and three hundred Italian officers on the day they arrived.

The officers were held in Vršac in a large POW camp. During the day they were used to repair roads and other infrastructure in the area. All the officers had learned that all enlisted men and NCOs were being released after "re-education," which lasted six months to a year. This was encouraging information.

Later they were moved to a military jail at Belgrade. Here they were interrogated about Nazi Party membership. Most Company Grade officers had no more connection with the Nazi Party than did other country's Company Grade officers had with the political leaders in their respective governments. If they had, they wouldn't be a company grade officer. In fact, many of the field and general grade officers had great dislike for politics in the military. They especially resented the micromanaging of military planning by politicians!

At any rate, they were all interrogated about Party membership and real and made up atrocities. If after several sessions with their equivalent of the GESTAPO or NKVD, if you didn't admit to one of these real or fictious atrocities, you were given an early version of waterboarding until you broke. If you didn't break and sign an admission, you were taken out the door to the yard and shot. No trial. From the waterboarding, out the door, and shot.

Noack, being much older than the other officers, discussed this execution procedure and encouraged them to agree after waterboarding to signing their damned fake confessions. He told them there would be plenty of records to prove later that they did or did not participate in war crimes. The great majority agreed. Of the five thousand eight hundred officers, about two hundred were summarily executed; five thousand six hundred signed. All were convicted by Tito's court on 06 December 1949 AD as war criminals. They were sentenced to an additional twenty years in prison at hard labor. They were again back on the roads of Yugoslavia working out their sentences; better than being dead.

By 1952 Germany was well on its way to rebuilding under the leadership of Chancellor Konrad Adenauer, the first Bundeskanzler. It was a smaller republic as Germany was divided into West and East in the Communist zone and Berlin was still a divided city inside the Communist zone.

West Germany was improving. As Noack had told his men, their duty was to help rebuild. He had never imagined that the country he loved would be divided in two. He thought back how the Soviets had taken half of Poland with no real assistance in the fight. Politically Stalin was no fool. Noack didn't know it at the time, but he actually agreed with U.S. General George Patton, who after the war until his death thought that the Americans had more in common with the Germans than we did with the Communists, specifically Russians. Patton had worked closely with German civic leaders in his area. Patton had things running very smoothly. In fact, many of the German civic leaders had become friends with their former enemy. This worried senior American officers at SHAEF. Since details of Patton's traffic accident were removed from all archives and there was no autopsy done on General Patton's body, we may never know the facts.

Noack thought, after talking at length earlier with the LTC who was in command of the American camp where he surrendered his men that not following the promises of the American pamphlet was not the LTC's fault. He knew the LTC had no choice, no more than he had when he was recalled into the Army in 1939. Politics and economic considerations, as usual!

15

RELEASE AND RETURN TO A DIVIDED GERMANY

In January, 1952, AD, the first POWs of the approximate fifty-four hundred who survived with Noack were exchanged for truckloads of building supplies. Tito needed these supplies for Yugoslavia's infrastructure and got them from West Germany. So, after almost six and a half years at hard labor in Yugoslavia and almost twelve years and five months since being recalled into the German Army, Herr Kurt Noack was among the first exchanged by Yugoslavia. Noack and the other lucky former POWs were debriefed in West Germany and reclassified and issued civilian identification. They were taken to Marburg in Hesse, Germany, for hospitalization. The balance of the approximate fifty-four hundred men who survived (an estimated two hundred were executed and about two hundred died from illnesses), were all exchanged for infrastructure material by the end of 1953. Noack's best guess of the total released was about fifty-four hundred men. A handful of higher ranking officers were handed over to other Allied authorities for further investigation. About two hundred had died of natural causes due to poor diets and physical labor beyond their physical capability.

Herr Kurt Noack was released from the Marburg Hospital in late May, 1952, and with his new civilian identification was allowed to cross into East Germany and return to Cottbus, but his family had already started their move west. He went back to Berlin where he had some friends and relatives. His time back in Cottbus and a visit to Guben convinced him that the East was much worse off than the West.

While at Checkpoint Charlie in West Berlin on the way back west, Herr Noack asked an American NCO on a smoke break, "What is a SNAFU?" Laughing loudly, the NCO replied, "I can't tell you, Opa; it's a military secret."

While working day labor jobs here and there for small wages, he kept moving toward Schotten where he was told his wife,

Johanna, Hans-Jürgen, his son, and Hannelore Heidi, his daughter, were. He arrived in Schotten circa early 1956. Germans with family separated by the new East and West Germany border were still allowed to travel back and forth. Noack thought it best for his family to be in the West permanently. His friends still in the East kept him informed through traveling relatives that it was getting worse.

He and Johanna selected a quaint, old town, Friedberg (Hesse) which had been walled centuries before as their new home. The move was completed in 1956. Hans-Jürgen was turning twenty-two and Hannelore was nearing fifteen. He had missed most of their childhood and adolescence but was determined to make a good home for them and especially for Johanna, who had kept his family together and safe.

As a Wehrmacht Heer veteran of World War I and World War II, he would get a small pension and all medical expenses for life. They eventually found a nice modern apartment in Friedberg (Hesse). Hans-Jürgen had completed school and followed in his dad's footsteps, becoming a government civil servant administrator.

He moved up over the years. He married LisaLotte and had children. His dad, Herr Noack, finally was told by an American soldier what SNAFU meant.

Hannelore remained with her parents and finished high school.

She worked for several years drafting for the coal mining office which was nearby. Eventually she went to work as an office clerk at the local Volkswagen dealership. Here she met Sergeant Robert Spangler in 1965. They dated and by fall, 1965, she was inviting him home for dinner with her parents, Herr Kurt and Johanna Noack. They were married in January, 1966. Sergeant Spangler was scheduled to rotate to his next Army assignment in December, 1966, so he arranged for his pregnant wife to fly back to Columbia, South Carolina, in September 1966. She was greeted at the airport by Shirley and Dennis Snyder, Sergeant Spangler's aunt and uncle. They took her to the home of Mr. and Mrs. Stephen D. Snyder, Sr., his grandparents. Hannelore was welcomed by his grandmother, Tracy LaLone Snyder, and made to feel welcomed. His grandfather was in an assisted living unit close by. Steve Snyder, Sr., was a hardworking man who had retired from three jobs. He and his wonderful wife had raised six children through two World Wars and a depression. He had just run out of steam as many of us eventually do. Hannelore fit right in and sensed the genuine love she received from the South Carolina relatives.

Hannelore gave birth to Francis Kurt Spangler on October 18, 1966. Her husband, his dad, was absent. She learned later he had been told of Frank's birth by a kind CWO, Mr. Freddie L. King, who had taken the time to locate this Recon Sergeant. He found Spangler in a snow covered ditch late at night in the field near Fulda.

Two months later while all slept at the Snyder home, Sergeant Spangler arrived after driving from Charleston, where his plane from Germany had landed. After a week's leave and a chance to visit with his wife, his baby boy, and many other relatives, especially his grandfather, the three Spanglers left by Volkswagen to Fort Rucker, Alabama, for his last duty assignment.

The Noack family in Friedberg naturally missed their

daughter, but the contingencies of life took over and time moved on. Hannelore was comforted knowing that her brother and the family were living close together and she kept in close contact.

Marburg Hospital in West Germany after the reclassification center

Marburg Hospital, Oberleutnant Noack seated first on left

Reclassification Center. Fellow Wehrmacht officers, released Yugoslavian POWs, at West German reclassification center prior to reclassification, were released by Tito in exchange for building materials from Bundeskanzler Konrad Adenauer, January 1932.

Official West German photo of civilian Herr Kurt Noack, age fifty plus, for required identification card

16

REUNIONS WITH KAMERADEN

The former Oberleutnant Kurt Noack made inquiries about survivors of all of the Divisions he had served in and assisted other veterans in setting up monthly and annual get togethers. When not engaged in these activities, he read articles, essays, and books about the events of the war. He was absolutely stunned when he learned that Poland had not attacked Germany, that it had been a faked event by a Blacks Ops specialist assigned to this task by the SD in Berlin. He read of the atrocities that were rumored at the end of the war. He had been so busy trying to save the men for whom he was responsible and himself that he hadn't paid any attention until now. Like any religious person, he was deeply saddened. He also knew that the great majority of Heer and Waffen SS Disposition Line troops had not done these things. It did become evident later that a small percentage of Heer and a larger percentage, maybe thirty percent, of Waffen SS line troops were transferred away from their normal combat assignments to serve under the Political SS associated with the SD. The SD organization was full of people who make up the seven to eight percent of psychopaths, sociopaths, and just plain evil men and women that cut across all professions, races, religions, and countries. The average German had no part in these things; neither did the average soldier, sailor, or airman, no more than the average Allied family took part in the thousands of rapes, murders, and thefts by the same types of deranged people who were in their branches of the military (the seven to eight percent of humans).

Noack reflected on the Jews who had died and grieved as others who believed in God did. He also hoped that younger Germans would understand that the great majority of Wehrmacht personnel were not involved in anything other than serving their country, just like the majority of Allied soldiers, with the exception of Stalin's troops. Their lives were at stake as well: Stalin would kill them if they did not carry out orders, just as Hitler had killed our officers, NCOs, and enlisted when he was displeased. Politicians and ministers can make lofty speeches about moral duties not to obey orders. Not in the former Soviet military or in the Third Reich's military. You were shot. He wondered how many of these holier than thou politicians and ministers would have refused orders and walked to the wall? He said, "Not many I'm sure."

These things were on both Noack's and other veterans' minds. They discussed these things at their reunions. They did enjoy knowing that these Kameraden had survived and they exchanged their stories.

By 1973 West Germany was doing much better than East Germany economically and was becoming a powerhouse economically on the European scene. The wall had gone up in 1961 separating families, eight years after "Uncle Joe" Stalin had died.

American children during World War II had been taught to refer to Stalin as Uncle Joe, our friend. It appeared that Soviet policies toward the outside world weren't improving very much but had internally as fewer of their own citizens had been slain since Stalin's death.

Bob and Hannelore Spangler with young Frank in tow arrived in Friedberg, Hesse, in 1973 to visit her parents and other relatives. It was Bob's first visit since rotating out to Fort Rucker, Alabama, in December 1966. It was his wife and son's second visit. While there, it was like old times with Bob and the former Wehrmacht Oberleutnant taking long walks after dinner and talking about World War II. They also talked indoors about the pictures he had annotated and he asked for more details of events they had discussed in the past. Noack was very pleased that his young grandson sat listening as the two men went over his grandfather's experiences. Before they left for the States, as Bob was now an Assistant Professor of Psychology at East Tennessee State University and had classes to prepare for the upcoming semester, he renewed his promise to Kurt Noack. He would give all the photos, notes, and tapes to young Frank when he was old enough. All were kept in a safety deposit box at his bank.

At the end of the ten day visit with the Noacks, the three Spanglers departed. Hannelore and Frank made other visits, but

Bob only saw Kurt and Johanna one other time in 1977.

Johanna and Kurt Noack died in the 1980s and did not live to see the reunification of Germany. They are buried in Friedberg (Hesse.)

Herr Kurt Noack greets former veterans at a party at area hotel. Kameradin all!

Sgt. R.S. Spangler driving from Ray Barracks to home of Herr Kurt Noack, late Fall 1966

Former Wehrmacht officers enjoy a lunch together in Friedberg (Hessen) area.

17

UNIDENTIFIED PHOTOS

If your family member or friend served in the Wehrmacht Heer, Luftwaffe, Kreigs/Marine, or Waffen SS Disposition Units, contact: The German Government Federal Records Office, Military Archives, Postfach 79024 Freiburg, Wiesentalstrasse 10, 79115 Freiburg, Deutchland; Phone 071 47817-0 OR a Veteran's publication: Arbeidsgemeinschaft fur, Kameradenwerke und Tradstionerbande, e.v., Tirebringer Strasse 12-16, D-70178 Stuttgart, Deutchland; Phone 00-49-711-22CO620

If you found a photo of a family member or friend who was in France, Holland, or Denmark, contact Military Archives in your nation's capital. We have no photos from Poland or Yugoslavia.

EPILOGUE

Herr Kurt Noack died in 1982. He never served with or met the four below listed authors of sincere autobiographical works that give readers the sense of fear, the emotions, the hopelessness ingrained from massive combat, and the determination of soldiers depending on their superior officers for wise choices. Herr Noack died before these four books were published, but he described similar fears, emotions and fatalities during his interviews in 1965, 1966, and 1975. Herr Noack and these authors tell it as experienced by fellow humans, not the crisp, forensic descriptions as presented by many historians.

In his candid memoirs, *Blood Red Snow* (page 4), Koschorrek describes the difficulties in writing an accurate chronology after many years have passed. This book is also from the perceptions of how a recalled World War I soldier in 1939 experienced the events of World War II until 10 May 1945. He then experienced being a POW until 1952. We were helped by the opportunity for the first author to go over the timeline of events, details from 1939 to May 1945 as a soldier and as POW from May 1945 to 1952 during interviews in 1965 and 1966 and again in 1973 with Herr Noack.

In this last interview with Herr Kurt Noack in 1973 special attention was paid to the last mission of the 22nd Infantry Division from Crete in September 1944 to January 1945 in Sarajevo, the special mission to Šabac by Noack and a squad of eight while the main body of the 22nd Infantry Division went south of Sarajevo on one last rescue mission of trapped Wehrmacht soldiers, while Noack and his squad were ordered to Sabac, then returned to Visegrád. Then to Sarajevo to find the 22nd Division had left for Austria ten days earlier.

Former Oberleutnant Kurt Noack agreed with timelines, battles, the run through Yugoslavia toward the Drina River, Visegrád, Sarajevo, and withdrawal toward Austria in an attempt to catch up with the 22nd Infantry Division.

Literary license used was in the description of the three days of R & R in Visegrád after Šabac . All that Noack would say was that he had a feeling that the worst was yet to come, and he wanted his squad to relax, rest, and enjoy their young lives with friendly civilian allies. He wanted his men to be in better physical and mental condition when they left Visegrád. They were.

The dismay felt by Johann Voss (pages 205 and 206), *Black Edelweiss*, as he described it, on an annual Memorial Day visit to a cemetery honoring friends; fallen soldiers when he saw a disturbance by young German Peace movement people and the press. It was an unexpected insult from fellow Germans taken stoically. Even the Bundeswehr soldiers were restricted from attending for several years, until the Zeitgeist changed. Noack had also described feelings of dismay.

In 1965 and 1966 Noack, unaware of the incident -- or at least Herr Noack didn't mention it -- he expressed the same disdain for current German youth in the sixties and the Bundeswehr soldiers he had observed and talked to in Hesse. In fact, he had made a statement about the 1965 era German soldiers in Germany so quickly that later his son, Hans-Jürgen, had to translate it for our notes. Roughly the World War I and World War II soldier and Heer Officer from late 1943 to 10 May 1945 said, "Current German soldiers I see in Hesse aren't good enough either to carry the jock straps of the Wehrmacht Heer or Disposition Front-line troops." He had opined that earlier about the SD, who dressed like soldiers but were not. When questioned about this in 1973, he stated he wasn't comparing the two in terms of SD psychopathology, only both would be weak front line soldiers.

Bidermann, in his realistic and informative memoir, *In Deadly Combat* describes "unnerving scenes" in early May 1945 experienced by Wehrmacht front-line troops evacuating by ship and unarmed Luftwaffe Air Transports. Many of the unarmed planes were shot down by Soviet fighters. The older married troops who were being evacuated first were killed.

Three ships full of evacuating troops that could not keep up with the convoy docked in Sweden (page 285). The "neutral" country of Sweden turned these soldiers over to the Soviets.

Noack, in a different theatre of operation in May 1945, describes similar feelings. He felt despair for his men and himself after he had marched his men over five hundred miles, surrendered to the U.S. Army when he could not break through to the 22nd Infantry Division, and then he and his men were turned over to the Yugoslavian Partisans.

In his comprehensive World War II memoir, *The Forgotten Soldier*, Sajer (pages 392-393), describes the feeling shared by most of the soldiers near the end. Victory was out of the question, but they felt they couldn't be defeated. There was a sense of general unease throughout the soldiers.

This was exactly what Oberleutnant Noack was trying to explain to the young Major upon arrival at Sarajevo in January 1945. He was threatened with a firing squad for defeatism. Noack was spared by volunteering for a highly dangerous mission to Šabac with a small squad of eight men.

Although Kurt Noack was always in a different theatre of operation than the above-mentioned soldiers/authors and he never met or communicated with them, he verbalized similar feelings, concerns, and perceptions of his troops, fatigue, sentiments, their hopes in 1965 and 1966 interviews and re-affirmed in 1973.

In 1977 Bob met Hans-Jürgen in Friedberg and drove to Stuttgart. They saw factories and did sightseeing and enjoyed a few beers. Herr Kurt Noack enjoyed his grandson, Frank, and his daughter, Hannelore's company back in Friedberg (Hesse).

From 1956 until his death in 1982, Herr Noack attended veterans' lunches and dinners. The men discussed their experiences but also tried to understand all the revelations that were being documented as time moved on. Some refused to believe this new information; most were just flabbergasted and saddened.

Front-line soldiers, Allied or Axis, with the exception of the Communists were generally not active political party members and the German Landsers and the American GIs had one thing in mind when they got away from combat for a few hours or a few days, and it wasn't politics. The overwhelming majority focused on beer, liquor, and women. In 1973, Noack said, "In terms of politics, the exception were some higher ranking General Grade Officers who got to their positions through politics. This happened in all armies throughout the ages.

The General Grade Officers who came up through the military, not politics, resented these ass kissing backstabbers who climbed the ladder over better men in World War II. Military careers were limited or ended due to lightweight political risers. Regular Wehrmacht higher ranked non-political Generals hated the political SD in Berlin and the other Generals who sold out and caved into political expediency. Whether in the Army Heer, the Disposition Divisions, the Navy, or the Luftwaffes, the higher ranking non-political officers resented the insanity and micromanagement of military matters by politicians totally unfit to override military decisions that were planned with recent input from Field Commanders.

But they did override decisions. Unfortunately for soldiers, sailors, marines, and airmen in most countries, in 1973 they still do!

ABOUT THE AUTHORS AND
NOACK/SPANGLER FAMILY EVENTS:
AS TIME WENT BY (1965 -2020)

Hans-Jürgen Noack (1934-2006), walking in Hesse, circa 2003

Opa and Oma Noack, 1977, another visit from Franky as promised in 1966

Bill and Bob in England, New Years Eve 1998, served together in Co. F, 124th Inf., FNG on active duty in 1953

Karl-Heinz Freund, Frank Spangler, and Hannelore Noack Spangler-Freund, New Orleans LA 2018

Robert and Franky

A postcard from Oma and Opa Noack to six-year-old Frank (Francis Kurt Spangler) in 1973

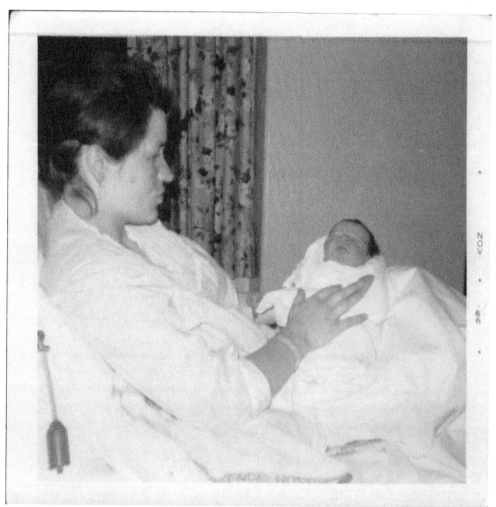

Hannelore Noack Spangler and her one day old son, Francis Kurt Spangler, 19 October 1966

Franky's first visit to Opa Kurt Noack and Oma Johanna as promised

Hannelore welcomed in South Carolina, September 1966. From left front, Dorothy Rozier, Lore holding Debbie Metz, Shirley and Stephanie Snyder, Grandmother Snyder, Terri Metz (daughter of T/Sgt Webby Rozier who was hit after crossing the Remagen Bridge in March 1945), Betty Spangler, and Jeanette Stier

1967 – Frank E. Spangler (stepfather of Robert, a Corporal in the Americal Division who fought Japanese on Solomon Islands), Franky at eight months, Hannelore, Alisa, and Robert Spangler seated.

1968 – Robert, Franky, Lore, Robby, and Alisa

Christmas 1969 with Grandmother Theresa Snyder, Robert, Franky, and Hannelore

Hans-Jürgen Noack with Robert Spangler in Stuttgart, Germany, circa January 1978

Hans-Jürgen Noack and Robert Spangler, Circa January 1978

Last photo received by Robert S. Spangler of former Oberleutnant Kurt Noack in Freidberg, Hesse, at dining table, circa late January 1979. He died in 1982.

Robert S. Spangler and Carol Victoria Spangler at New Years Eve dinner in England, December 31, 1998

Francis Kurt and Christy McMullan Spangler visit with Grandmother Betty (Catherine Elizabeth Snyder Spangler) for her birthday, October 21, 1999

Francis Kurt and Robert S. Spangler II with Dad at the Daytona 24 hour race in 2002

Frank K.'s older sister, Alisa Spangler-Miller, with picture of their great grandparents, Theresa LaLone and Stephen D. Snyder, circa 2002

Robert S. and Carol V. Spangler congratulate Francis (Frank) Kurt and Christy McMullan Spangler on receiving their Masters degrees at East Tennessee State University

Herr Karl-Heinz Freund and Frau Hannelore Noack Spangler-Freund, circa September 2018

FKS working on dedication; hotel on the Danube in Vienna, 12 January 2014

The Danube – the Sava joins it in Belgrade

GLOSSARY

- Abwher: Intelligence

- BN: Battalion: Five or six companies organized together under a Field Grade Officer.

- Disposition Troops: Divisions of Waffen SS line troops.

- GHQ: Higher headquarters.

- HQ: Company headquarters.

- HHC: Headquarters and headquarters company, Bn or higher.

- Kammandantur: A central location of German Occupation Forces, GHQ, in Kolding, Denmark.

- NCO: Non-commissioned officer.

- NKVD: Soviet Secret Police, evolved into KGB.

- OKH: Highest German Regular Army headquarters.

- OKW: Wehrmacht highest headquarters (Army, Navy, and Air Force).

- OIC: Officer in Charge.

- OSS: Office of Strategic Services, created by William J.

Donovan, evolved into CIA.

- SD: Third Reich's Secret Police, Gestapo. Became dominated by the SS (*The Rise and Fall of the Third Reich*, page 274). Under Heinrich Himmler the pollical, paramilitary group expanded significantly. In Noack's opinion, ours, and others, one unit of the Waffen SS who were elite combat soldiers trained to fight on the line along with the Heer and did. Another small unit of soldiers assigned from the Waffen SS as bodyguards, except for a small percentage of men who by direct order or as volunteers served with the political psychopaths in the commission of the atrocities, including the Holocaust. The Third Unit of the Waffen SS, the Death's Head Battalions was involved from day one in the concentration camps, slave labor, and gassings. This guilt, stain, and dishonor should not be laid on the overwhelming majority of the elite combat troops and those who were only bodyguards if they did not volunteer for illegal duty or executions. "Noack's opinion, ours, and stated in *Black Edelweiss*, pp 201-203)."

- SHAEF: Supreme Headquarters Allied Expeditionary Forces.

- SNAFU: Situation Normal All Fu**ed Up.

- XO: Executive Officer.

- T O & E: Table of Organization and Equipment

BIBLIOGRAPHY

Bidermann, Gotlob Herbert: *In Deadly Combat: A German Soldier's Memoir of the Eastern Front*, Lawrence, Kansas, 2000

Koschorrek, Gunter K.: *Blood Red Snow*, London, 2002

Sajer, Guy: *The Forgotten Soldier*, Washington, D.C., 2000

Shirer, William L.: *The Rise and Fall of the Third Reich*, New York, 1960

Voss, Johann: *Black Edelweiss*, Bedford, Pennsylvania, 2002

FOR OUR SON, FRANK

CHRISTMAS WITH MON AND KARL-HEINZ
GERMANY
DECEMBER 2018

FRANCIS KURT SPANGLER
BORN: 18 OCTOBER 1966, COLUMBIA, SC
DIED: 26 APRIL 2019, TAMARAC, FL

WITH LOVE, MOM AND DAD

Made in the USA
Columbia, SC
04 September 2024

41649090R00222